Editor
Lorin E. Klistoff, M.A.

Managing Editor
Karen J. Goldfluss, M.S. Ed.

Editor-in-Chief
Sharon Coan, M.S. Ed.

Illustrator
Kathy Marlin

Cover Artist
Brenda DiAntonis

Art Coordinator
Kevin Barnes

Imaging
James Edward Grace

Product Manager
Phil Garcia

Product Developer
Quack & Co.

Publishers
Rachelle Cracchiolo, M.S. Ed.
Mary Dupuy Smith, M.S. Ed.

Bible Crafts

Author
Mary Currier

Teacher Created Materials, Inc.
6421 Industry Way
Westminster, CA 92683
www.teachercreated.com
ISBN-0-7439-7101-9
©2002 Teacher Created Materials, Inc.
Reprinted, 2004
Made in U.S.A.

Table of Contents

Introduction

Learning about the Word of God and God's love is an important task for Christian children. Sunday school teachers, classroom teachers, and parents will find this craft book to be a valuable resource in accomplishing this goal. Each fun, and simple, craft is based on a Bible verse. Children can discover that learning Bible verses can be fun!

The book is divided into four seasonal sections with the season listed in the top right corner of each page. This feature will make finding a craft to relate to a specific holiday or timely Biblical topic much easier.

The craft projects have been developed with the goal of making them simple and easy to use. They are all paper projects that are quick and simple, with reproducible patterns included. Children will have fun making such crafts as goodie bags, mobiles, paper plate art, puppets, baskets, bookmarks, and picture frames, to name a few.

Enjoy watching children create fun, wonderful crafts as they better understand the Word of God and the love He has for each and every one of us.

Personal Attendance Chart

I rejoiced with those who said to me, "Let us go to the house of the Lord." (Psalm 122:1)

This chart is perfect to use to record attendance for a month of Sunday school or for a 5-day Vacation Bible School program. If used for Sunday school attendance, print dates on the top five spaces. If used for Vacation Bible School, print the days of the week in the spaces.

Directions

1. Color the church on page 5.

2. Color and cut out the five cars.

3. Print your name in the space provided.

4. The chart can be taped flat to a wall. Or, fold on the dashed lines to make the church stand up.

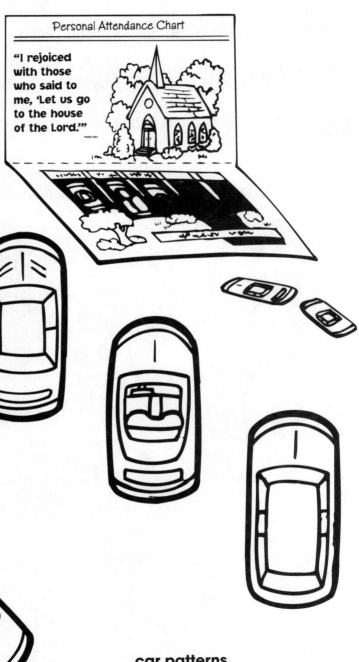

car patterns

Offering Plate

Each man should give what he has decided in his heart to give, not reluctantly or under compulsion, for God loves a cheerful giver. (2 Corinthians 9:7)

This plate makes it fun to collect money to give to God! We should all learn to give willingly and happily to God for God has given us many things.

Directions

1. Color and cut out the pattern.
2. Fold on the dashed lines.
3. Apply glue to the tabs, and fasten to form a box shape.

*Optional: Glue on lightweight cardboard.

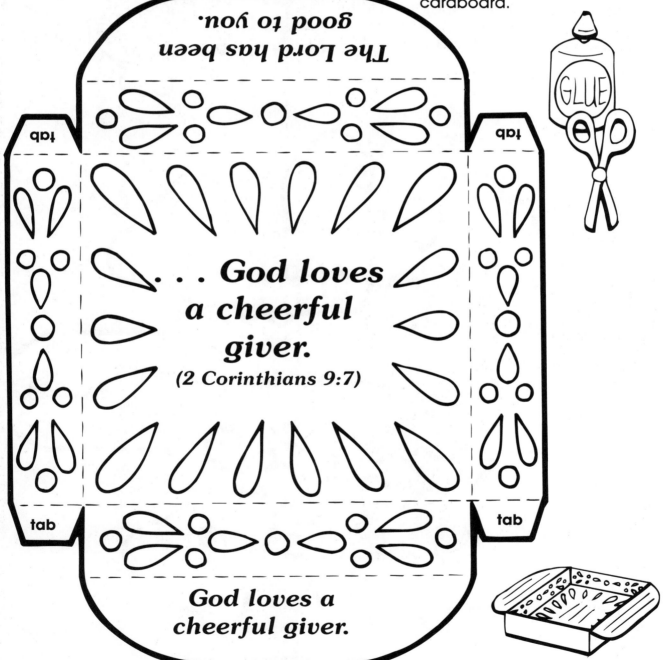

tab   tab

The Lord has been good to you.

. . . **God loves a cheerful giver.**
(2 Corinthians 9:7)

tab   tab

God loves a cheerful giver.

Faithful Turtle

I have fought the good fight, I have finished the race, I have kept the faith. (2 Timothy 4:7)

This turtle can remind us each to always be a good Christian. If we do kind deeds each day and follow God's law, we will win the Christian race.

Directions

1. Color and cut out the pattern.

2. Fold on the dashed lines.

3. Apply glue to the tab, and fasten to the area marked with an *. The turtle should look rounded and sit up.

"Work for God" Circle

Whatever you do, work at it with all your heart, as working for the Lord, not for men.
(Colossians 3:23)

What a great way to remind us to do what we are asked to do! If we pretend it is God who asks us to do something, we can work hard and quickly to please Him and others.

Directions

1. Color and cut out the patterns.

2. Insert a brass fastener into the black dot in the boy. Then, insert into the black dot in each leg.

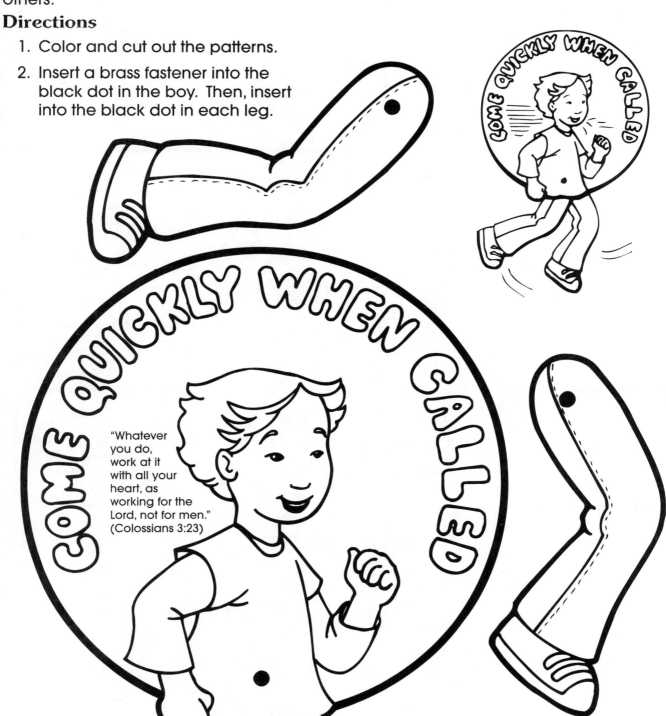

Words of Wisdom

Instruct a wise man and he will be wiser still; teach a righteous man and he will add to his learning. (Proverbs 9:9)

This owl is a fun way to learn words of wisdom to live by.

Directions

1. Color and cut out the owl pattern and strips. Remember, cut the slot on the owl, too.

2. Glue the slide on the back side of the owl over the slot.

3. Insert the strips in the slide to read them on the owl.

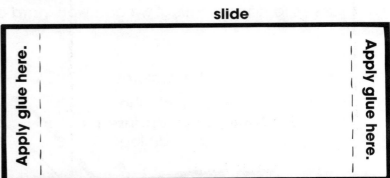

slide

Apply glue here.

Apply glue here.

back

Glue slide over slot.

WORDS OF WISDOM

Cut this slot out.

THINK, THINK, THINK!

14

Words of Wisdom

Verse Strip

"Create Your Own Message" Strip

"Instruct a

wise man

and he

will be

wiser still;

teach a

righteous man

and he

will add

to his

learning."

(Proverbs 9:9)

_____

_____

_____

_____

_____

_____

_____

_____

_____

_____

_____

_____

_____

_____

_____

A "Fruitful" Table Decoration

But the fruit of the Spirit is love, joy, peace, patience, kindness, goodness, faithfulness, gentleness, and self-control. Against such things there is no law. (Galatians 5:22–23)

This decoration is a wonderful way to remind others to live with these nine important virtues in their lives.

Directions

1. Color the leaves and the rings around the grapes.

2. Cut out on the bold lines.

3. Spread glue on the colored part of the grapes. Sprinkle on granulated sugar. Shake off excess.

4. Glue the decoration to a large sheet of construction paper. Write "the fruit of the spirit" all over the background.

5. Set it in the center of a table for all to admire.

* Optional: Use glitter instead of sugar.

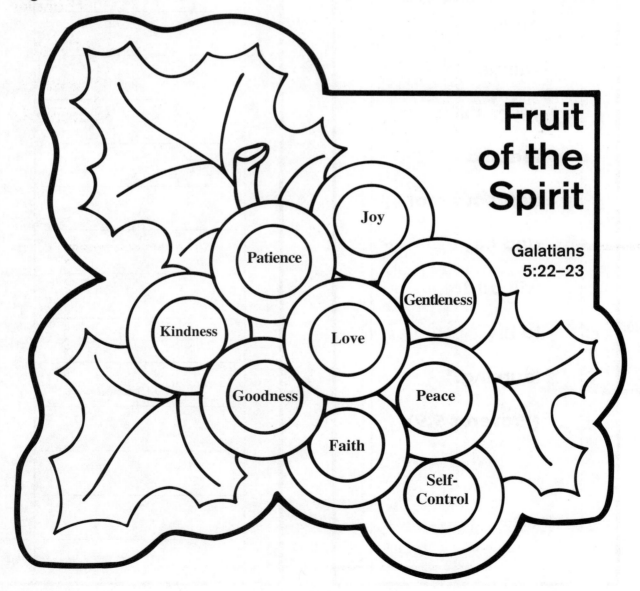

Encourage "mint" Candy Dish

Let us not become weary in doing good, for at the proper time we will reap a harvest if we do not give up. (Galatians 6:9)

What a nice way to motivate and encourage others! This candy dish is fun to make and can remind us and others to follow God's laws.

Directions

1. Color and cut out the pattern on the bold lines.

2. Fold on the dashed lines.

3. Apply glue to the tabs, and fasten to form a box shape.

4. Fill the dish with mint candies.

Have a Piece of Candy

Everyone Needs a Little Encourage "Mint"

tab

tab

tab

tab

Let us not become weary in doing good, for at the proper time we will reap a harvest if we do not give up. (Galatians 6:9)

Prayer Rounder

". . . Pray to the Lord . . ." (Acts 8:24)

This Prayer Rounder can remind us of the many people and things we should pray for!

Directions

1. Color the pattern below and write your prayer request on the lines on page 19.

2. Cut out the patterns. Be sure to cut out the window below.

3. Insert a paper fastener in the middle of the patterns.

4. Turn the circle to remind you of things you can pray for.

Cut out.

PRAY TO THE LORD (Acts 8:24)

Pray Without Ceasing

18

Prayer Rounder

PRAY
TO
THE
LORD

PRAY
TO
THE
LORD

Listen and Learn Owl Puppet

. . . *let the wise listen and add to their learning . . .* (Proverbs 1:5)

We can always learn more, and this owl is a great reminder of that! It can help us remember to learn as much as we can to help others and be good Christians.

Directions

1. Color and cut out the patterns.

2. Glue them on a lunch sack to create a puppet.

3. Use the puppet to ask yourself and others about the kinds of things good and smart Christians do.

BE WISE

BE WISE

20

"Treat" Others Kindly Basket

. . . always try to be kind to each other . . . (1 Thessalonians 5:15)

This basket makes a nice gift for anyone needing a little cheering up or encouragement.

Directions

1. Color the patterns.
2. Cut them out on the bold lines.
3. Fold on the dashed lines. Do not fold tabs.
4. Apply glue to the back of the squirrel, and glue it to the back of the Bible verse.
5. Apply glue on the back of the folded leaves, and glue them to the basket side (as shown) to create a box shape.
6. Glue on the handle by putting glue on the tabs.
7. Fill the basket with treats and give it to a special friend.

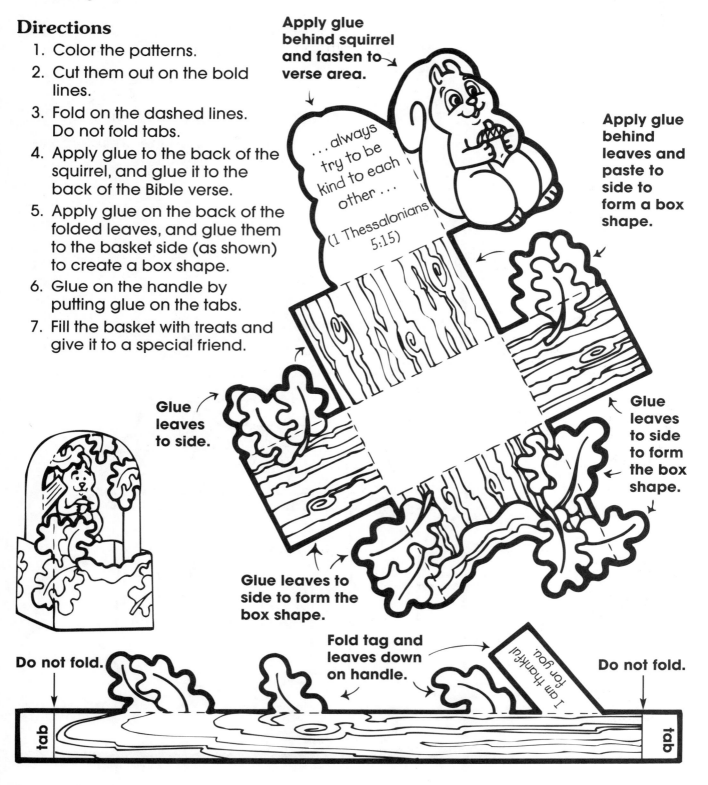

Apply glue behind squirrel and fasten to verse area.

. . . always try to be kind to each other . . . (1 Thessalonians 5:15)

Apply glue behind leaves and paste to side to form a box shape.

Glue leaves to side.

Glue leaves to side to form the box shape.

Glue leaves to side to form the box shape.

Fold tag and leaves down on handle.

I am thankful for you.

Do not fold.

Do not fold.

tab

tab

Church at Night

Surely goodness and love will follow me all the days of my life, and I will dwell in the house of the Lord forever. (Psalm 23:6)

This pretty picture is a nice symbol of what we can all hope to achieve someday—life in God's house, forever.

Directions

1. Color and cut out the church below and the sky scene on page 23.

2. Glue the church to the sky scene.

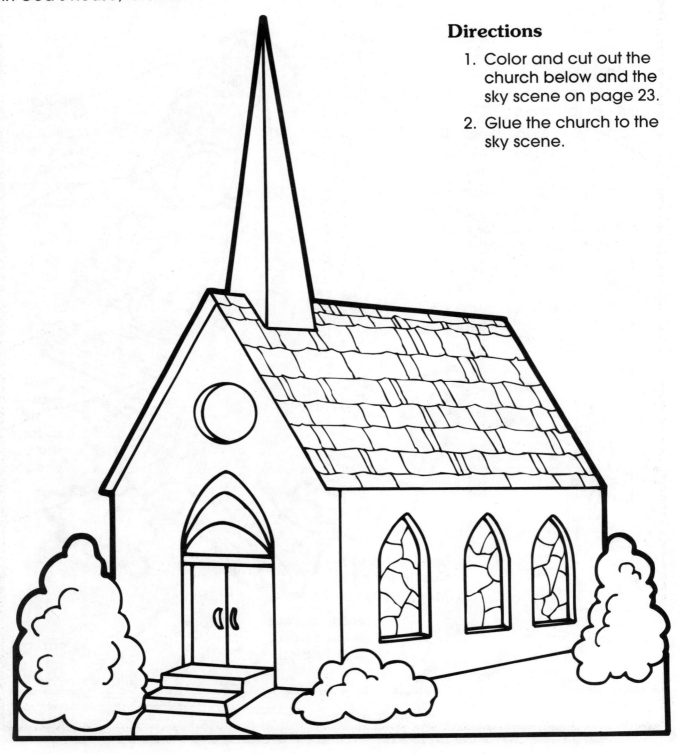

Church at Night

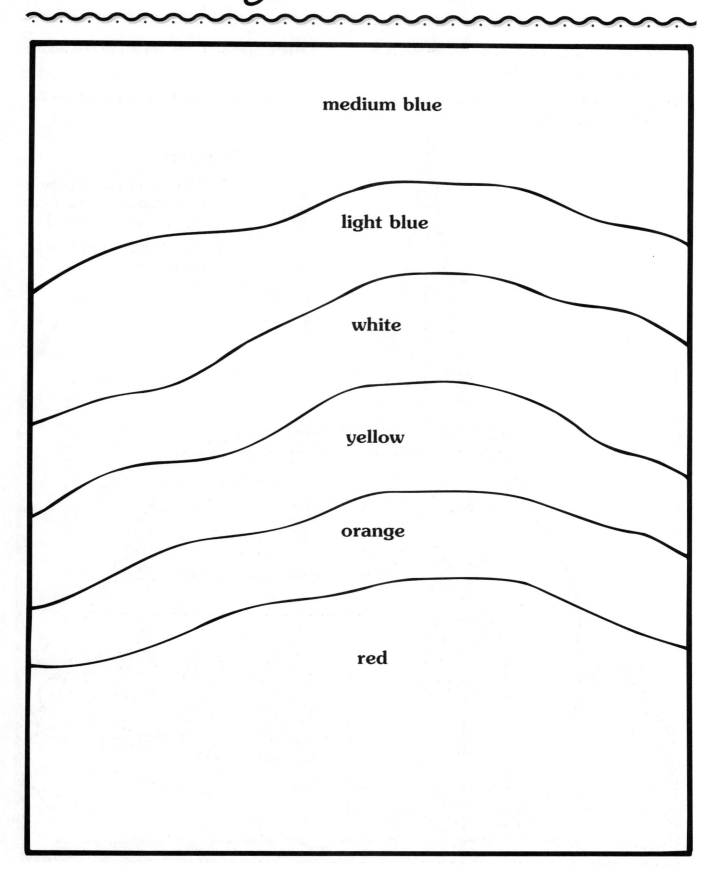

medium blue

light blue

white

yellow

orange

red

The Ten Commandments

Walk in the way that the Lord your God has commanded you, so that you may live and prosper . . . (Deuteronomy 5:33)

Display these Ten Commandment's stones on a refrigerator or door for all to see. What a wonderful daily reminder of God's laws!

Directions

1. Color the stone pattern around the edges.
2. Cut out on the bold lines.
3. Fold on the dotted lines.

*Optional: Glue the pattern onto lightweight cardboard. Glue small pebbles and sand around the edge.

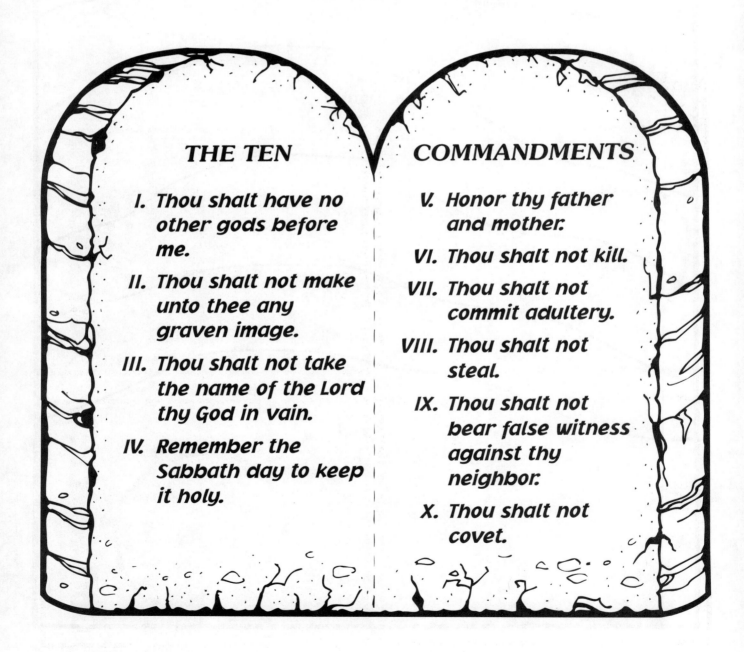

THE TEN

I. **Thou shalt have no other gods before me.**

II. **Thou shalt not make unto thee any graven image.**

III. **Thou shalt not take the name of the Lord thy God in vain.**

IV. **Remember the Sabbath day to keep it holy.**

COMMANDMENTS

V. **Honor thy father and mother.**

VI. **Thou shalt not kill.**

VII. **Thou shalt not commit adultery.**

VIII. **Thou shalt not steal.**

IX. **Thou shalt not bear false witness against thy neighbor.**

X. **Thou shalt not covet.**

Ten Commandments Flash Cards

And if we are careful to obey all this law before the Lord our God, as he has commanded us, that will be our righteousness. (Deuteronomy 6:25)

These flash cards make learning and memorizing the Ten Commandments fun and easy!

Directions

1. Color and cut out the number and answer cards on pages 25–28.

2. To use, show someone a number card. This person should try to quickly say the commandment that matches the number.

3. Use the answer cards to find the correct answer.

Number Cards

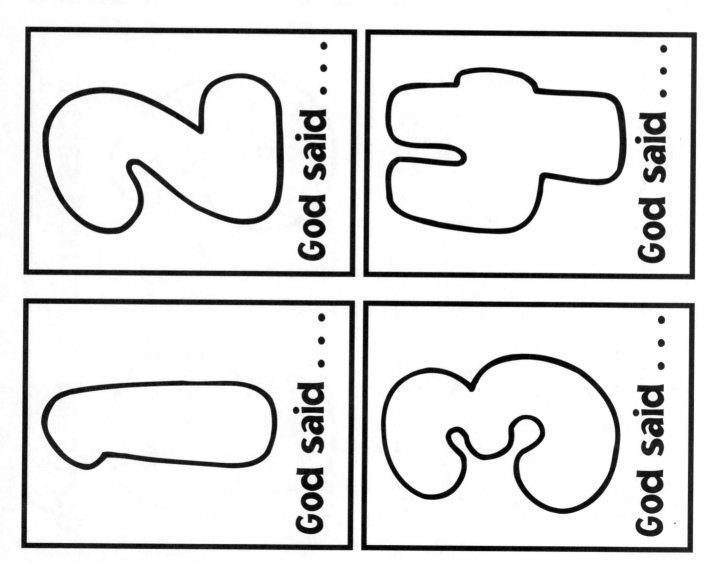

Ten Commandments Flash Cards

Number Cards *(cont.)*

Ten Commandments Flash Cards

Answer Cards

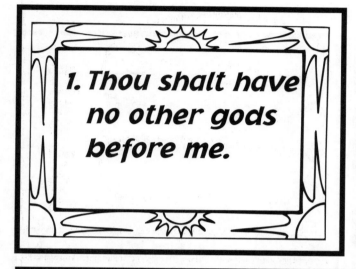

1. Thou shalt have no other gods before me.

2. Thou shalt not make unto thee any graven image.

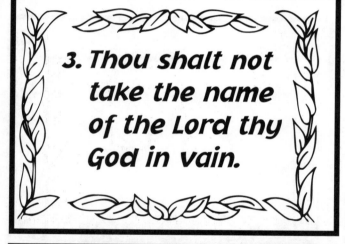

3. Thou shalt not take the name of the Lord thy God in vain.

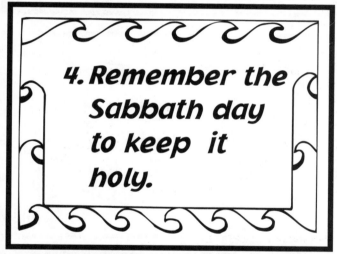

4. Remember the Sabbath day to keep it holy.

5. Honor thy father and thy mother.

6. Thou shalt not kill.

Answer Cards *(cont.)*

7. Thou shalt not commit adultery.

8. Thou shalt not steal.

9. Thou shalt not bear false witness against thy neighbor.

10. Thou shalt not covet.

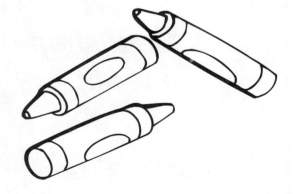

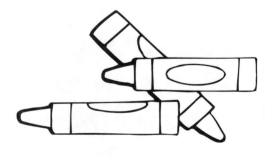

"Let Your Light Shine" Lamp

In the same way, let your light shine before men, that they may see your good deeds and praise your Father in heaven. (Matthew 5:16)

This lamp can help us remember to always let our lights shine for Jesus!

Directions

1. Color the bottom of the circle yellow. Color the lamp on page 30 any color you desire.
2. Cut out both patterns.
3. Insert a brass fastener into the center dot of the lamp.
4. Insert a brass fastener into the center dot of the circle.
5. Turn the circle to turn the light off and on.

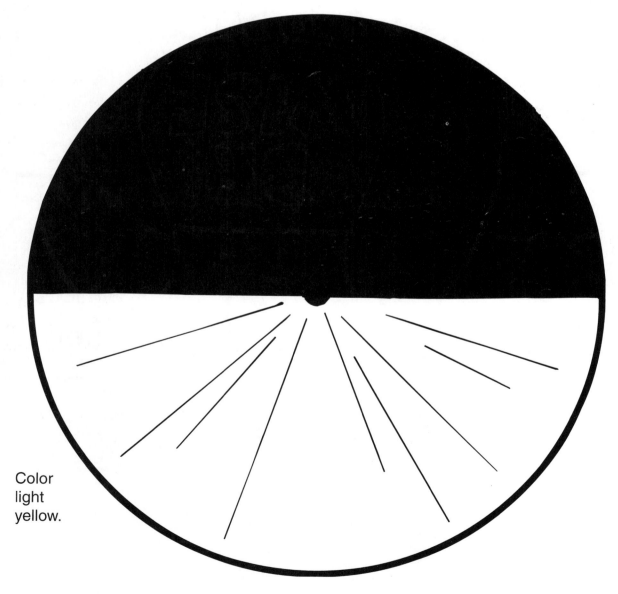

Color
light
yellow.

"Let Your Light Shine" Lamp

LET YOUR LIGHT SHINE

LET YOUR LIGHT SHINE

LET YOUR LIGHT SHINE

"In the same way, let your light shine before men, that they may see your good deeds and praise your Father in heaven." (Matthew 5:16)

"Money for Others" Bank

What good will it be for a man if he gains the whole world, yet forfeits his soul? . . .
(Matthew 16:26)

This bank makes a great project to save money for the poor.

Directions

1. Color and cut out the pattern.
2. Fold dashed lines.
3. Apply glue to tab A, and glue to area marked with an *.
4. Then put glue on the bottom tabs, and overlap to form a box.
5. Glue the top of the bank as shown.

   (**Note:** This should be made with heavy, sturdy paper to hold coins.)

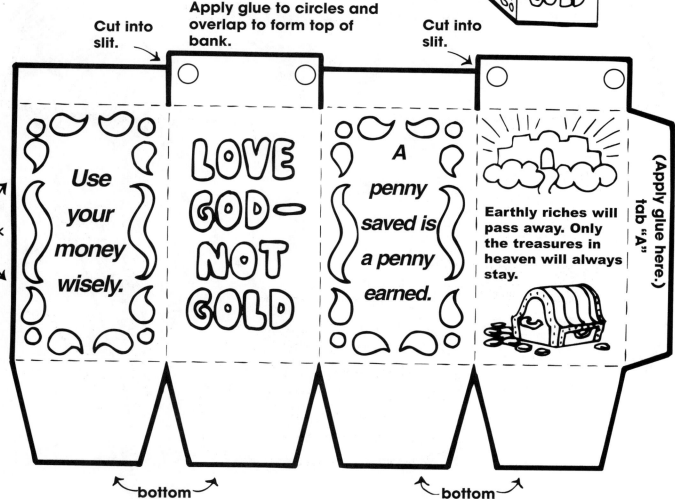

Cut into slit.

Apply glue to circles and overlap to form top of bank.

Cut into slit.

Use your money wisely.

LOVE GOD — NOT GOLD

A penny saved is a penny earned.

Earthly riches will pass away. Only the treasures in heaven will always stay.

(Apply glue here.) tab "A"

bottom tabs

bottom tabs

Toothbrush Reminder

Wash yourselves and make yourselves clean . . . (Isaiah 1:16)

We should thank God for our healthy bodies every day. This toothbrush is a great way to remind us to take care of our very special teeth!

Directions

1. Color and cut out the pattern.

2. Fold on the dashed lines.

3. Apply glue to the tab, and fasten to form a handle.

*Optional: Punch holes where shown. Insert a string and tie. Hang up the toothbrush to remind you to brush your teeth.

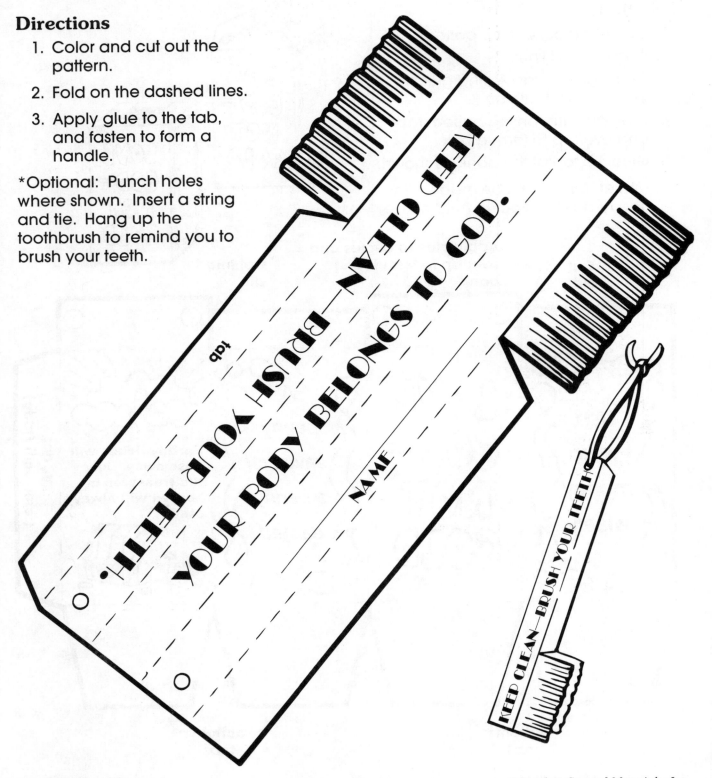

"Make Each Day Count" Circle

"The grass withers and the flowers fall, but the word of our God stands forever."
(Isaiah 40:8)

This circle traces the short life span of a dandelion. It can remind us that we need to live good Christian lives everyday for life is short.

Directions

1. Color and cut out the pattern on this page and page 34.

2. Insert a brass fastener into the center dot of pattern A. Then insert the brass fastener into the center dot of pattern B.

Life is short— seek God early!

"A"

"The grass withers and the flowers fall, but the word of our God stands forever."

(Isaiah 40:8)

"Make Each Day Count" Circle

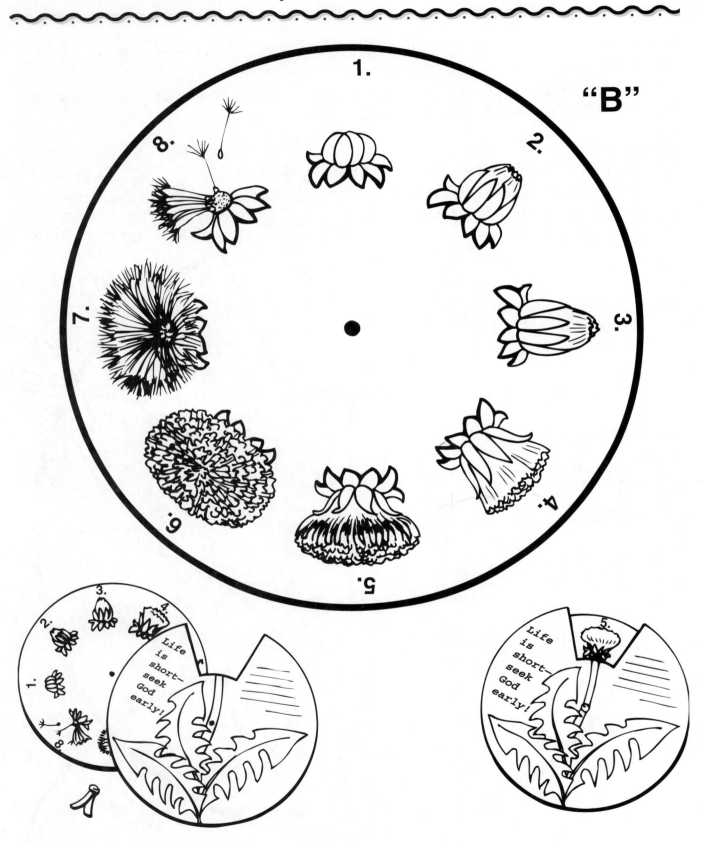

"B"

34

Lions' Den Diorama

I thank and praise you, O God of my fathers: You have given me wisdom and power, you have made known to me what we asked of you, you have made known to us the dream of the king. (Daniel 2:23)

This diorama makes learning about Daniel and our one true God lots of fun!

Directions

1. Color and cut out the pattern on this page and the patterns on page 36.

2. Fold on the dashed lines to make the characters stand.

3. Place a small cardboard box (such as a shoe box) on its side.

4. Cut a hole in the top to represent the place where Daniel was thrown into the den of lions.

5. Decorate the inside of the box to look like a lions' den. You can draw rocks or a wall of rocks on the sides of the box. You can put small, real rocks on the "floor" of the den.

6. Set the patterns in the box.

7. If desired, add more lions.

Lions' Den Diorama

36

Daniel and the Lions Finger Puppets Autumn

Daniel answered, "O king, live forever! My God sent his angel, and he shut the mouths of the lions. They have not hurt me, because I was found innocent in his sight . . ."
(Daniel 6:21)

These puppets are perfect to use to retell the story of Daniel in the lions' den.

Directions

1. Color and cut out the patterns.

2. Tape each to fit snugly around your finger.

"God Bless Our Home" Plaque

. . . *"The Lord has blessed the household . . ."* (2 Samuel 6:12)

This plaque will look nice hanging anywhere! It can remind us of God's presence in our homes.

Directions

1. Color and cut out the pattern.

2. Fold on the dashed lines.

3. Apply glue to the tabs, and fasten to form a 3-D frame.

4. Use tape to attach a short length of string. Hang.

"Our Daily Bread" Plaque

"Give us today our daily bread." (Matthew 6:11)

This kitchen plaque is a nice reminder of the Lord's Prayer. It can also remind us to be thankful of all the wonderful food God gives us.

Directions

1. Color and cut out the pattern.

2. Glue the pattern to cardboard or poster board. Cut it out again.

3. Punch a hole at the top of the plaque. Insert a string, and tie a loop.

4. Hang the completed plaque.

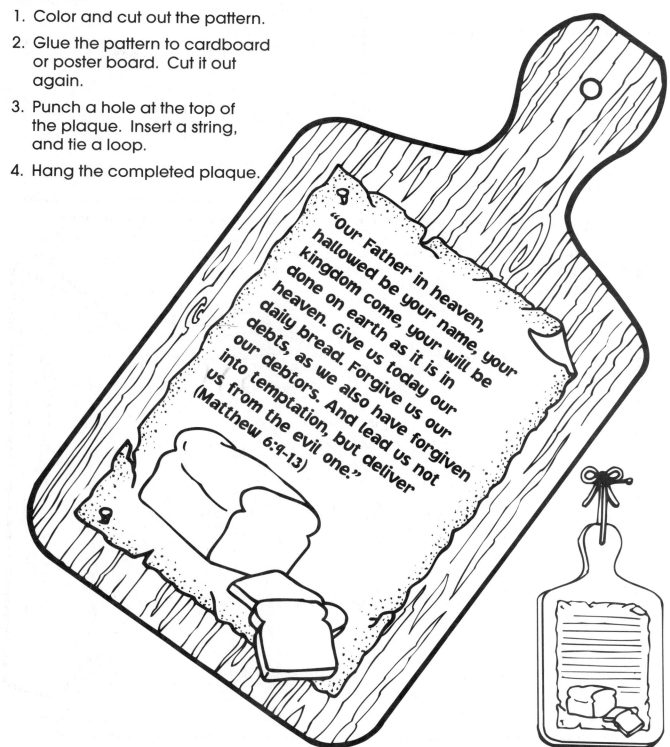

"Our Father in heaven, hallowed be your name, your kingdom come, your will be done on earth as it is in heaven. Give us today our daily bread. Forgive us our debts, as we also have forgiven our debtors. And lead us not into temptation, but deliver us from the evil one." (Matthew 6:9-13)

You Are What You Eat

They ate till they had more than enough . . . (Psalm 78:29)

This activity is a great way to learn how to keep our bodies and minds healthy—both physically and spiritually.

Directions

1. Color the patterns on this page and the pattern on page 41.

2. Cut out the patterns following the dashed lines.

3. Tell the following story:

   You need to eat a well-balanced meal to be healthy. A good meal consists of whole grains, meat, vegetables, and fruits. Milk is a better drink than soft drinks.

   We also need to be "healthy" spiritually. Jesus teaches us how to live a "well-balanced" life. We can obey Jesus to live a good Christian life.

   Just as we must eat good foods to make our physical bodies to grow, so we must also read and obey God's law to keep our "spiritual bodies" healthy.

   Junk food never completely satisfies our hunger or gives our bodies what we need. These foods are "empty" foods. They do not make our bodies healthy.

   So be sure to keep your body healthy by feeding it healthy foods, and remember to keep your "spiritual body" healthy by living according to God's law

4. Glue the healthy foods to the plate pattern on page 41.

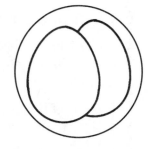
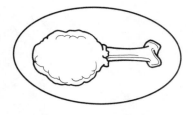

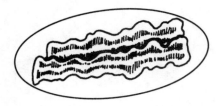

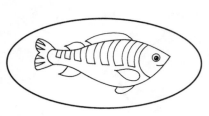

40

You Are What You Eat

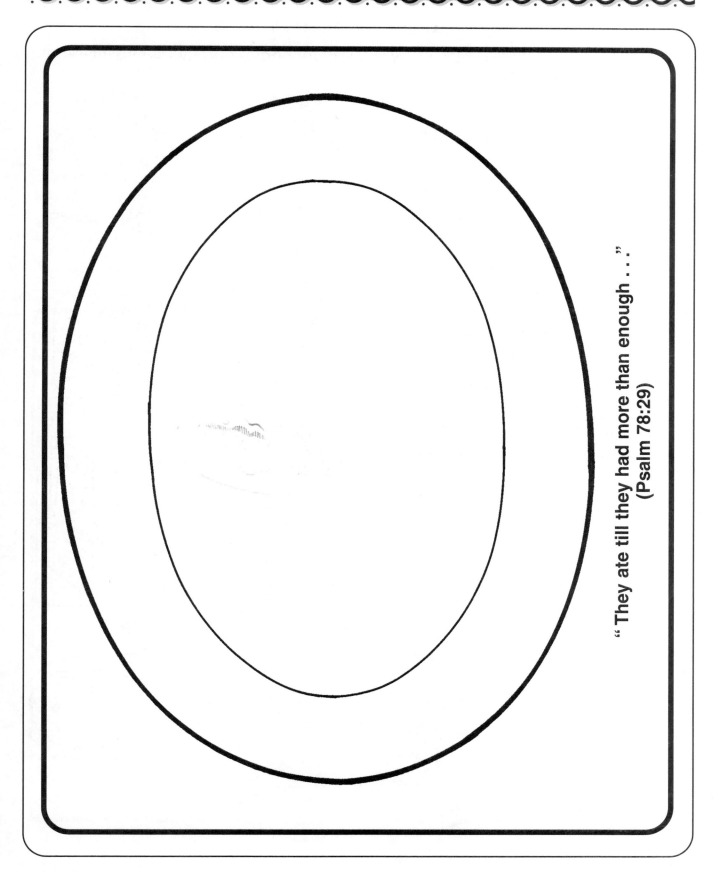

" They ate till they had more than enough . . ."
(Psalm 78:29)

All Need to Hear God's Word

"Therefore go and make disciples of all nations, baptizing them in the name of the Father and of the Son and of the Holy Spirit, and teaching them to obey everything I have commanded you. And surely I am with you always, to the very end of the age." (Matthew 28:19–20)

No matter where we live, we all need to hear and learn about God's Word.

Directions

1. Color the picture below.

2. Glue fluffed-up cotton balls in the dashed areas.

Optional: Make a collage of people all over the world who need to hear God's Word.

"God Sees Inside" Mirror

". . . The Lord does not look at the things man looks at. Man looks at the outward appearance, but the Lord looks at the heart." (1 Samuel 16:7)

Use this mirror to look deep into your heart. Do you like what you see? Does God?

Directions

1. Color and cut out the pattern.

2. Glue a 4" (10 cm) square of aluminum foil in the center of the mirror.

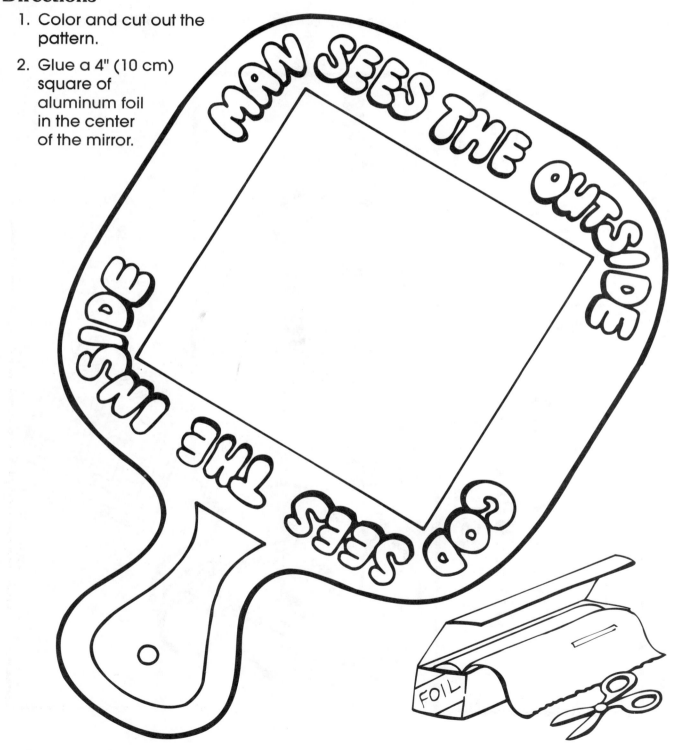

Motivating Bookmarks

Do your best to present yourself to God as one approved, a workman who does not need to be ashamed and who correctly handles the word of truth. (2 Timothy 2:15)

Use these bookmarks as a motivational tool or as gifts.

Directions

1. Color and cut out the patterns. (Markers work best as crayons may rub off onto the pages of the book.)

2. Keep the bookmarks or give them to friends.

#7101 Bible Crafts

44

©Teacher Created Materials, Inc.

"Pray Continually" Lamp Decoration Winter

Pray continually. (1 Thessalonians 5:17)

This lamp decoration is a great reminder to pray to God for the forgiveness of sins.

Directions

1. Color and cut out the pattern.
2. Punch a hole where shown.
3. Tie one end of a 12"–15" length of thread in the hole.
4. Tie the other end of the thread to 2–3 paper clips. (The paper clips are used as a weight when hanging the project.)
5. Place the end with paper clips over the top of the lamp shade.
6. Adjust the pattern to the desired place on the lamp.

Angel Picture Frame

The angel of the Lord encamps around those who fear him, and he delivers them.
(Psalm 34:7)

What a sweet frame to remind us that angels are guarding us!

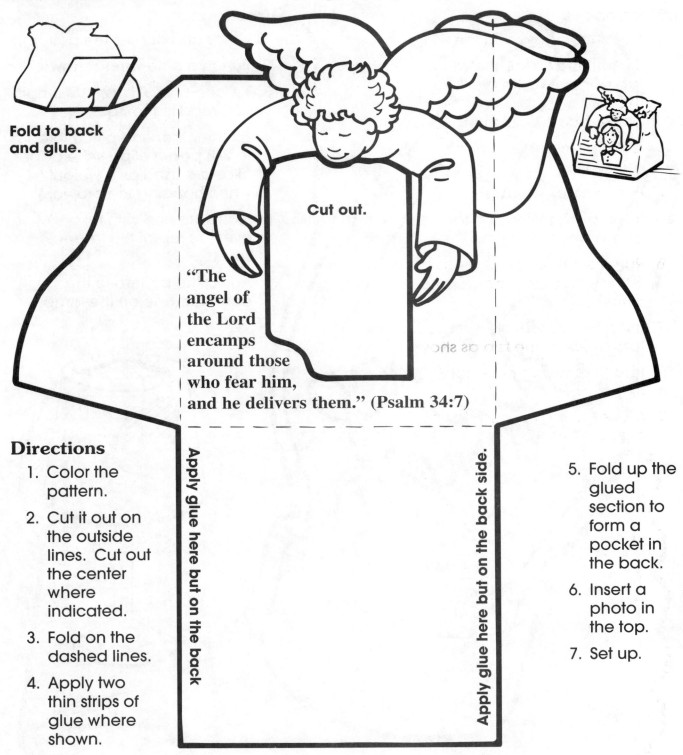

Fold to back and glue.

Cut out.

"The angel of the Lord encamps around those who fear him, and he delivers them." (Psalm 34:7)

Apply glue here but on the back

Apply glue here but on the back side.

Directions

1. Color the pattern.
2. Cut it out on the outside lines. Cut out the center where indicated.
3. Fold on the dashed lines.
4. Apply two thin strips of glue where shown.

5. Fold up the glued section to form a pocket in the back.
6. Insert a photo in the top.
7. Set up.

Movable Wings Angel

For he will command his angels concerning you to guard you in all your ways. (Psalm 91:11)

Moving this angel's wings is fun. It can remind us that God sends His angels to protect us.

Directions

1. Color the angel and the wings.

2. Cut out the angel, the wings, and the tab pattern on the bold lines. Glue them all on lightweight cardboard or poster board. Cut them out again.

3. Cut a slit in the bottom of the robe as shown.

4. Punch holes where shown.

5. Insert brass fastener in the holes of the angel, and then in the wings. Fasten.

6. Run a short length of string (about 4" or 10 cm) through areas marked with asterisks (*).

7. Bring the ends of the string down, and tape them to the tab as shown.

8. Insert the tab into the slot in the bottom of the robe.

9. Move the tab up and down to make the wings move.

God sends angels to help us!

Gift Tags

For the wages of sin is death, but the gift of God is eternal life in Christ Jesus our Lord.
(Romans 6:23)

These tags can be festive and spiritual. What a great way to make any gift special!

Directions

1. Color and cut out the tags.
2. Fold them on the dashed lines.
3. Punch a hole in each one.
4. Tie a ribbon through each hole, and tie to a package.

Christmas Candle

"She will give birth to a son, and you are to give him the name Jesus, because he will save his people from their sins." (Matthew 1:21)

This candle looks nice sitting on a table at Christmas. It can remind us of the one true Light in our lives.

Directions

1. Color and cut out the patterns.

2. Fold on the dashed lines.

3. Apply glue to the tab, and roll the pattern to form a tube shape.

4. Glue the two holly leaves under the Bible verse. Do not cover verse.

5. Fold and set up the candle.

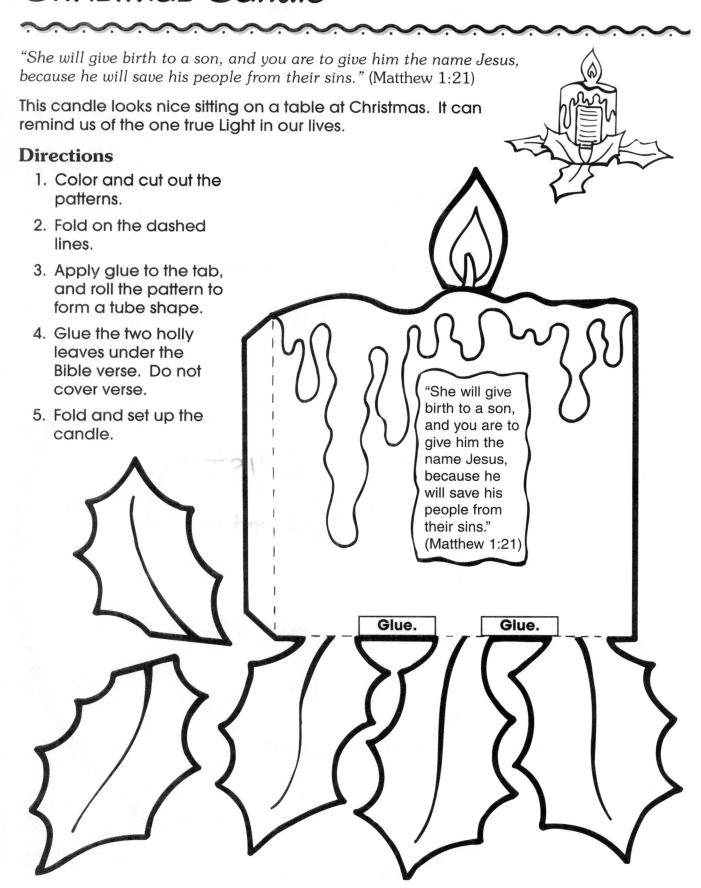

"She will give birth to a son, and you are to give him the name Jesus, because he will save his people from their sins." (Matthew 1:21)

Glue.   Glue.

Christmas Wreath

"The virgin will be with child and will give birth to a son, and they will call him Immanuel"—which means, "God with us." (Matthew 1:23)

This wreath is a great reminder of the true meaning of Christmas!

Directions

1. Make 2 copies of page 51.
2. Color and cut out the patterns.
3. Glue the ribbon, holly, and berry pieces to the wreath pattern as shown.

Christmas
—a time to remember Jesus Christ's birth

Christmas Wreath

Christmas Carolers

But the angel said to them, "Do not be afraid. I bring you good news of great joy that will be for all the people." (Luke 2:10)

These Christmas carolers are a cheery way to remind others of the joy of Jesus' birth.

Directions

1. Color and cut out the patterns on this page and page 53.

2. Apply glue to the tab. Fasten to the area marked with an * to form a cone shape.

3. Set up.

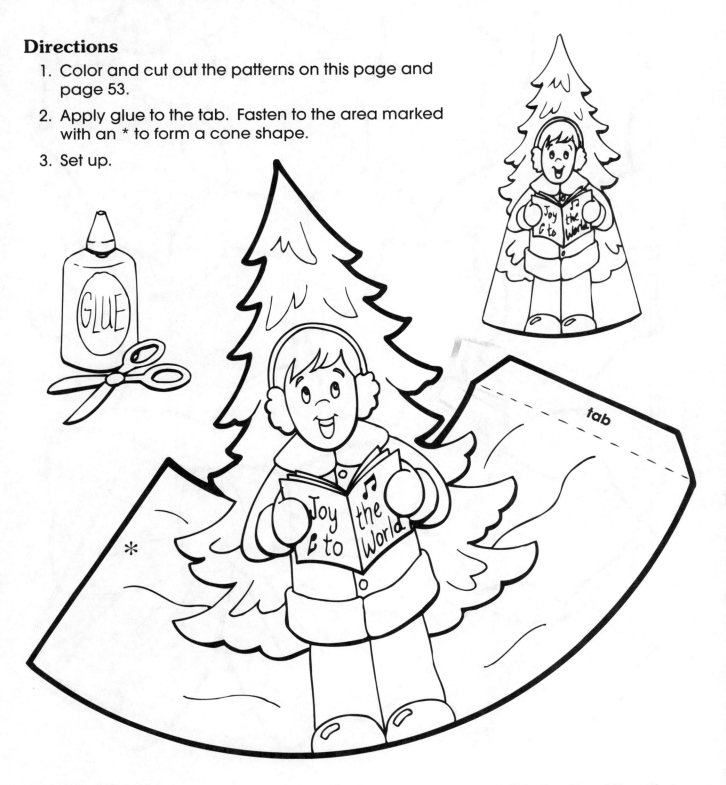

Christmas Carolers

53

Christmas Decoration

"Today in the town of Bethlehem a Savior has been born to you; he is Christ the Lord."
(Luke 2:11)

This little decoration is a festive way to remind others of our Savior's birthday.

Directions

1. Color the leaves and berries on the pattern.
2. Cut out the pattern.
3. Punch two holes where indicated by the black dots.
4. Fold on the dashed lines.
5. Apply glue to the tabs. Fasten to form a decoration.
6. Insert a 6"–8" (15 cm–20 cm) colored ribbon (or string) into the two holes. Tie and hang for all to enjoy.

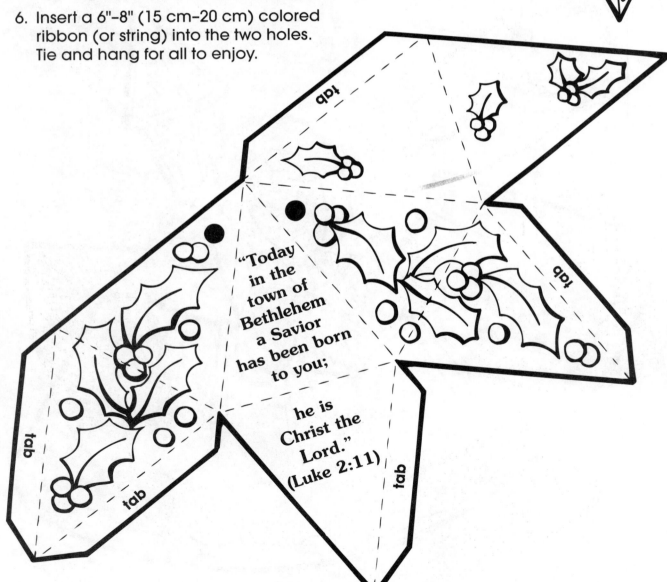

"Today in the town of Bethlehem a Savior has been born to you;

he is Christ the Lord." (Luke 2:11)

Christmas Place Cards

"Glory to God in the highest, and on earth peace to men on whom his favor rests."
(Luke 2:14)

These decorative place cards are a great way to remember Christ at your table!

Directions

1. Color and cut out the patterns.
2. Print names on the cards where shown.
3. Apply glue on the tabs.
4. Roll the patterns as shown.
5. Place each one on the table at the place setting.

May God's peace be with you always.

The gift of God is eternal life.

Name

Apply glue here.

Wishing You a Blessed Christmas

Wishing You a Blessed Christmas

Apply glue here.

Name

"Bells Are Ringing" Decoration

". . . celebrate with great joy. . ." (Nehemiah 8:12)

This bell is a super way to help celebrate the birth of Christ.

Directions

1. Color the borders around the bells.
2. Cut out the bells.
3. Fold each bell in half.
4. Glue the bells together, back to back, to form a 3-D decoration.
5. Tie a ribbon loop in the hole, and hang.

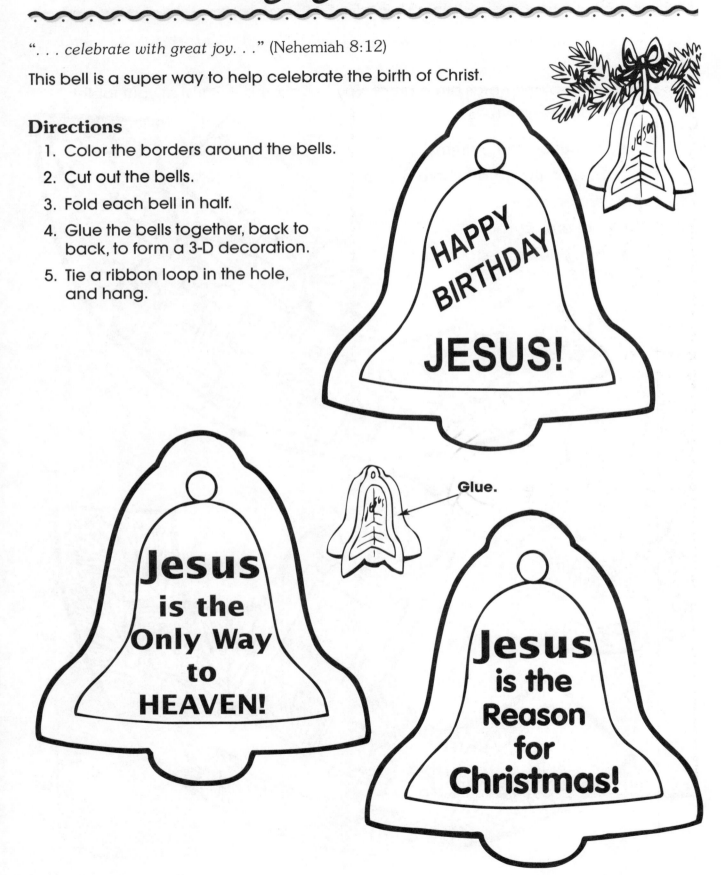

HAPPY BIRTHDAY JESUS!

Glue.

Jesus is the Only Way to HEAVEN!

Jesus is the Reason for Christmas!

"Tell the Truth" Pencil Holder

Apply glue here.

"The Lord detests lying lips, but he delights in men who are truthful." (Proverbs 12:22)

The Lord detests lying lips, but he delights in men who are truthful. (Proverbs 12:22)

What a nice way to remind us to always tell the truth!

Directions

1. Color and cut out the pattern.

2. Glue it around a frozen juice can.

57

"Help Others" Snow Scene

Even a child is known by his actions, by whether his conduct is pure and right.
(Proverbs 20:11)

What a kind deed this child is doing! This picture reminds us to do kind things—God and others will notice.

Directions

1. Color the boy and the shovel.

2. Cut out the picture. Glue it to a sheet of construction paper.

3. Apply a thin layer of glue over the snow on the ground and the snow in the shovel. Press fluffed-out cotton balls onto the glue to resemble snow.

4. Glue popped popcorn on the areas marked with an **X**.

"Even a child is known by his actions, by whether his conduct is pure and right." (Proverbs 20:11)

"God Made Winter" Snow Scene

It was you who set all the boundaries of the earth; you made both summer and winter.
(Psalm 74:17)

This beautiful winter snow scene is fun to make. It is just one example of beautiful things God has given us.

Directions

1. Color patterns below and on page 60.

2. Cut out on the bold lines. Cut the slit on the trees.

3. Fold on the dashed lines.

4. Slip both tree forms together to make the tree stand up.

5. Apply glue to the tabs on the church. Fold them together to form the building.

6. Apply glue behind the steeple but not yet on the tabs and glue together. Then put glue behind tab A and B on the steeple. Place it on top of the roof of the church where marked.

7. Set the project pieces on a small oval cardboard. Glue fluffed-up cotton balls on the tree branches and the on roof of the church.

8. Put a layer of glue on a 4"–5" (10 cm–13 cm) circle of heavy tagboard. Glue the church and tree to the base. Next, glue fluffed-up cotton balls to the base. If desired, sprinkle silver glitter over cotton "snow" or only use glitter with snow.

*Optional: Enlarge this project and use it for a table centerpiece. More trees can be added to the scene.

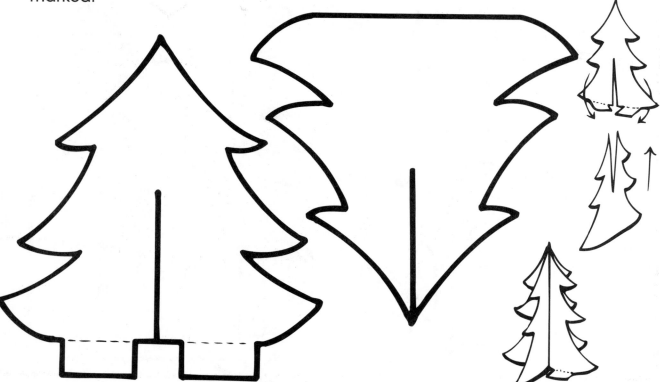

"God Made Winter" Snow Scene

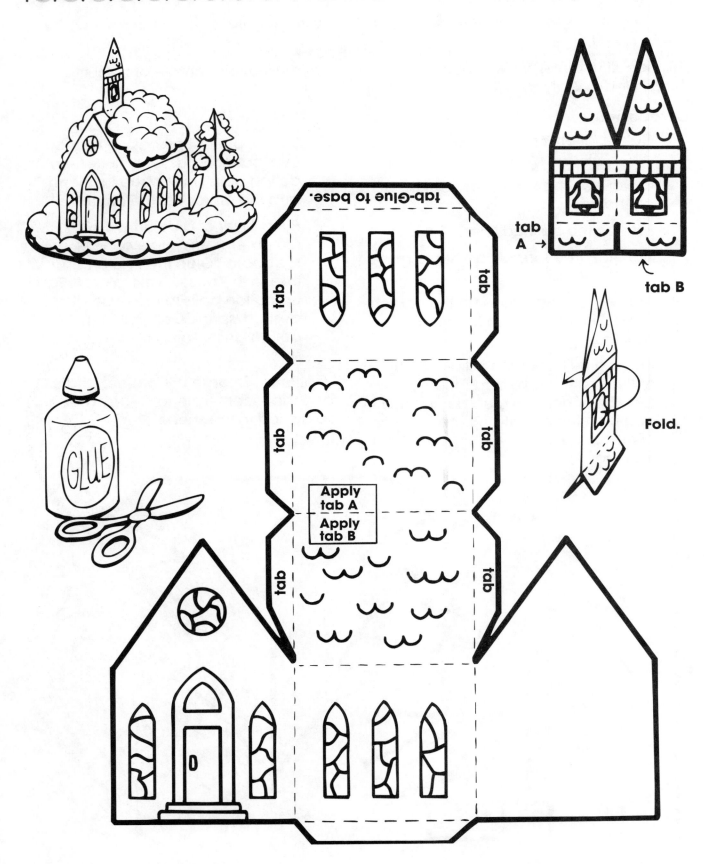

tab
A →

tab B

Fold.

tab-Glue to base.

tab

tab

tab

tab

Apply
tab A
Apply
tab B

tab

tab

GLUE

"We Serve the Lord" Decoration

". . . But as for me and my household, we will serve the Lord." (Joshua 24:15)

This decoration is perfect to remind us that God should be ever present in our homes.

Directions

1. Color the hearts.
2. Cut out all the patterns.
3. Glue the strips together at the tab.
4. Glue the hearts on the strip.
5. Hang.

" . . . But as for me and my house, we will serve the Lord." (Joshua 24:15)

Be it ever so humble, there's no place like home!

Valentine Cupcake Holder

Love the Lord your God with all your heart and with all your soul and with all your strength. (Deuteronomy 6:5)

This craft makes a great gift for Valentine's Day! It can remind us to love God always!

Directions

1. Color and cut out the pattern.

2. Fold on the dashed lines.

3. Apply glue to the tabs, and glue to form a box shape.

4. Set the cupcake in the box, and give it to a friend.

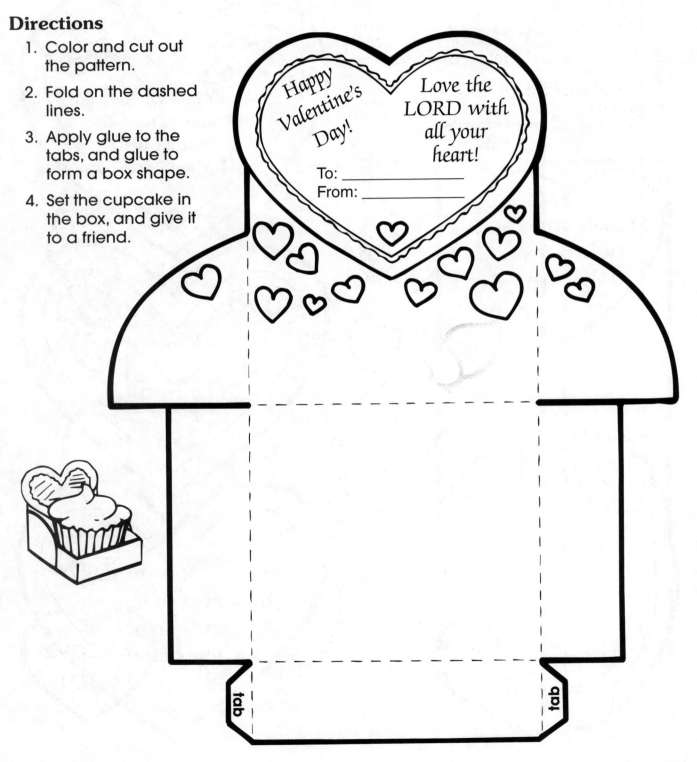

Happy Valentine's Day!

Love the LORD with all your heart!

To: _____
From: _____

tab

tab

Goodie Bag

A friend loves at all times . . . (Proverbs 17:17)

This little bag filled with goodies is perfect for any friend!

Directions

1. Color and cut out the patterns below.

2. Glue the colored patterns onto a small lunch sack.

3. Fill the sack with goodies, and give it to a friend or someone who needs cheering up.

Thank you for being my FRIEND!

JUST FOR YOU

Love the Lord with all your ♥

Thinking of You

I LOVE YOU!

Love Banner

. . . "I have loved you with an everlasting love . . ." (Jeremiah 31:3)

This banner can be hung proudly to let everyone know that God covers us all with love!

Directions

1. Color and cut out the banner.

2. Apply glue behind the area marked with an *.

3. Roll the top of the banner over a drinking straw as shown. Fasten with tape to hold.

5. Tie a 12"–15" (30 cm–38 cm) length of string on both ends of the straw to form a hanger. Hang for all to see!

Golden Rule Plaque

"So in everything, do to others what you would have them do to you . . ." (Matthew 7:12)

This little plaque is a wonderful reminder of God's Golden Rule.

Directions

1. Color and cut out the pattern.

2. Glue it on the cardboard. Cut it out again.

3. Punch out the holes as indicated.

4. Thread yarn through the holes. Tie a bow as shown. (Use a hair pin for a needle.)

Valentine Card

. . . *"Love the Lord your God with all your heart and with all your soul and with all your strength and with all your mind' (Deuteronomy 6:5); and, 'Love your neighbor as yourself.'"* (Luke 10:27)

This sweet card is a nice gift to a friend and a perfect reminder for us to think of God on this day, too!

Directions

1. Color and cut out the pattern.

2. Fold on the dashed lines.

3. Write names on the lines, and give it to a friend.

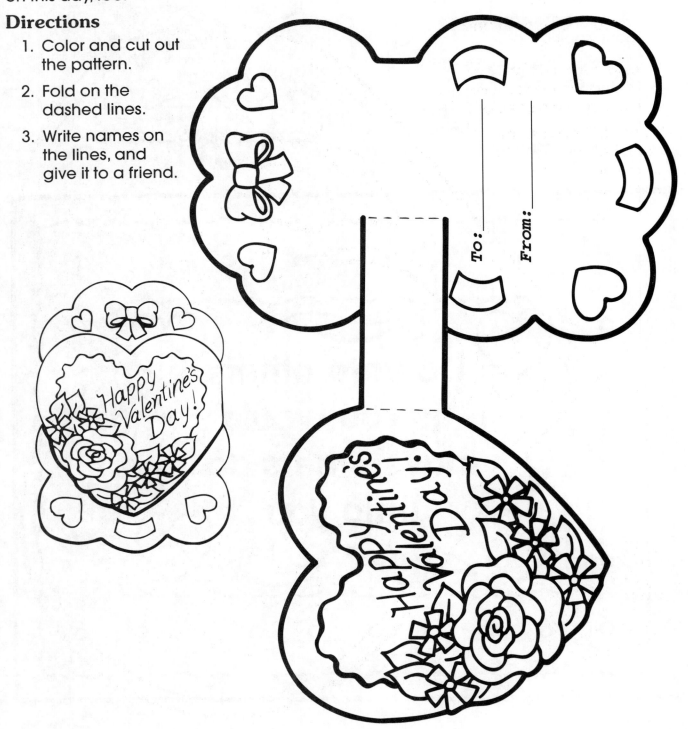

To:

From:

Happy Valentine's Day!

Happy Valentine's Day!

"Jesus Loves Me" Picture Frame

"As the Father has loved me, so have I loved you. Now remain in my love." (John 15:9))

This craft makes a perfect present for someone special!

Directions

1. Color the pattern.

2. Cut out the pattern and the center circle.

3. Tape your picture behind the circle. Give it to someone special.

*Optional: Tape a small mirror inside the hole, and glue the pattern on cardboard.

Cut out.

Pretty Wall Basket

And this is his command: to believe in the name of his Son, Jesus Christ, and to love one another as he commanded us. (1 John 3:23)

This little wall basket is pretty hanging on the wall!

Directions

1. Color and cut out the pattern.
2. Fold on the dashed lines.
3. Apply glue to the tab, and glue to form a basket.
4. Fill the basket with silk or dried flowers.
5. Punch a hole in the top to hang.

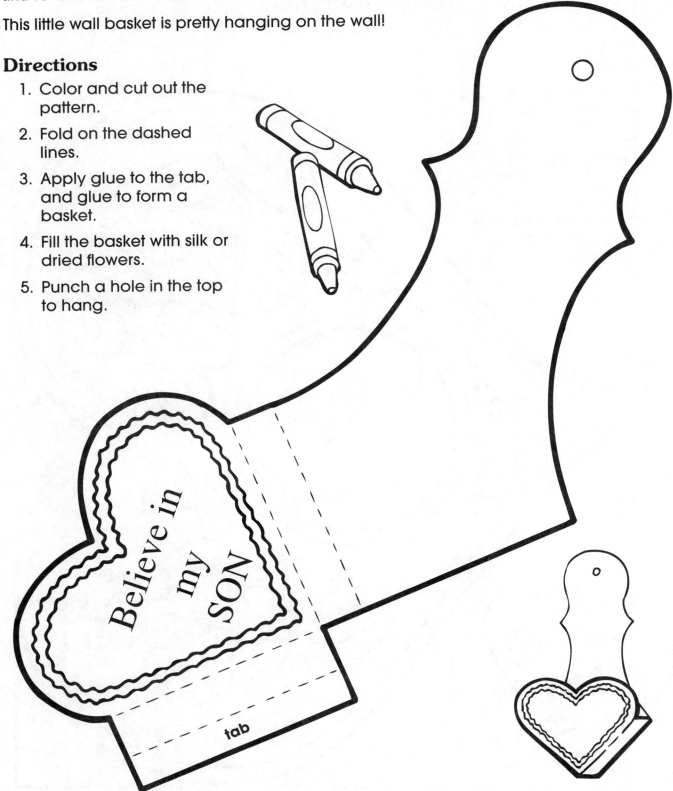

Believe in my SON

tab

Talking Fingers

We love because he first loved us. (1 John 4:19)

Signing "I love you" is a nice way to communicate with someone you love. Remember, Jesus loves you, too!

Directions

1. Color the pattern.
2. Cut it out on the outside lines. Cut the slits as shown.
3. Slip the slits together.
4. Stand it up.

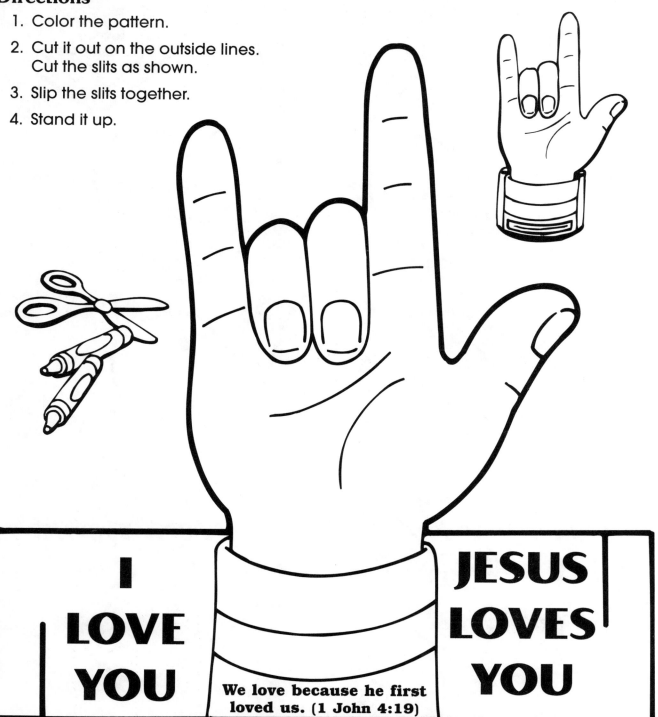

I LOVE YOU

JESUS LOVES YOU

We love because he first loved us. (1 John 4:19)

"God is Love" Mobile

God is love. Whoever lives in love lives in God, and God in him. (1 John 4:16)

This mobile is a great way to spread God's great love.

Directions

1. Color and cut out the patterns.

2. Punch holes where shown.

3. Use string to tie the hearts to the holes in various lengths as shown.

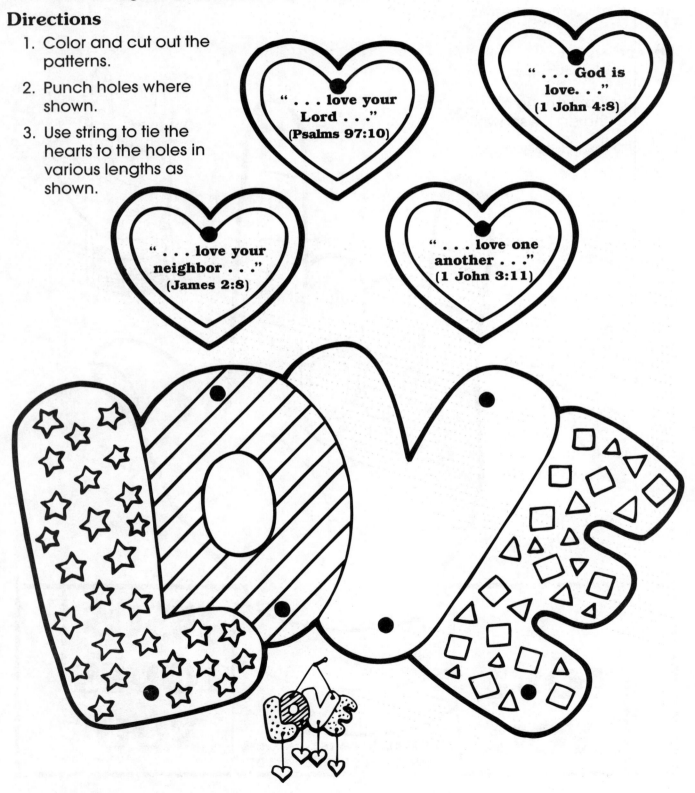

" . . . love your Lord . . ." (Psalms 97:10)

" . . . God is love. . ." (1 John 4:8)

" . . . love your neighbor . . ." (James 2:8)

" . . . love one another . . ." (1 John 3:11)

"Hearts of Love" Plaque

Dear friends, since God so loved us, we also ought to love one another. (1 John 4:11)

This cute wall hanging is a great way to help us remember to love each other!

Directions

1. Color the large heart red and the medium-sized heart pink. Leave the small heart white.

2. Cut out the hearts. Punch two holes in the large heart as shown.

3. Cut out five 1/2" (1.3 cm) squares of corrugated cardboard. Glue the squares on the large and medium hearts as shown.

4. Put glue on the top of each cardboard square.

5. Gently glue the medium heart on top of the large heart. (Make sure it is centered.)

6. Then set the small heart on top of the medium heart.

7. Tie a ribbon (about 12"–15") through. Hang and enjoy.

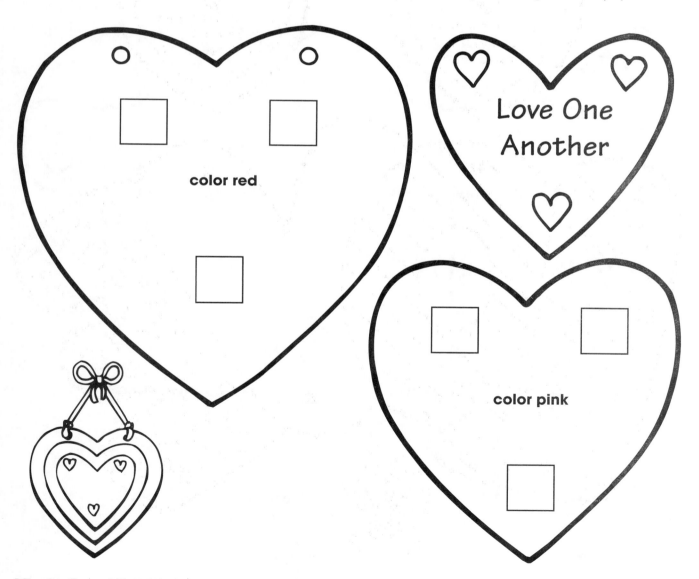

color red

Love One Another

color pink

"Bee" Sweet Cupcake Holder

How sweet are your words to my taste, sweeter than honey to my mouth! (Psalm 119:103)

This little cupcake holder is a sweet way to remind someone to "bee" kind!

Directions

1. Color and cut out the patterns.

2. Fold the dashed lines.

3. Place glue on the tabs, and form a box shape.

4. Frost a cupcake with yellow frosting to resemble the color of honey. Put the cupcake in the box.

5. Tape toothpicks to the bees, and stick them into the cupcake.

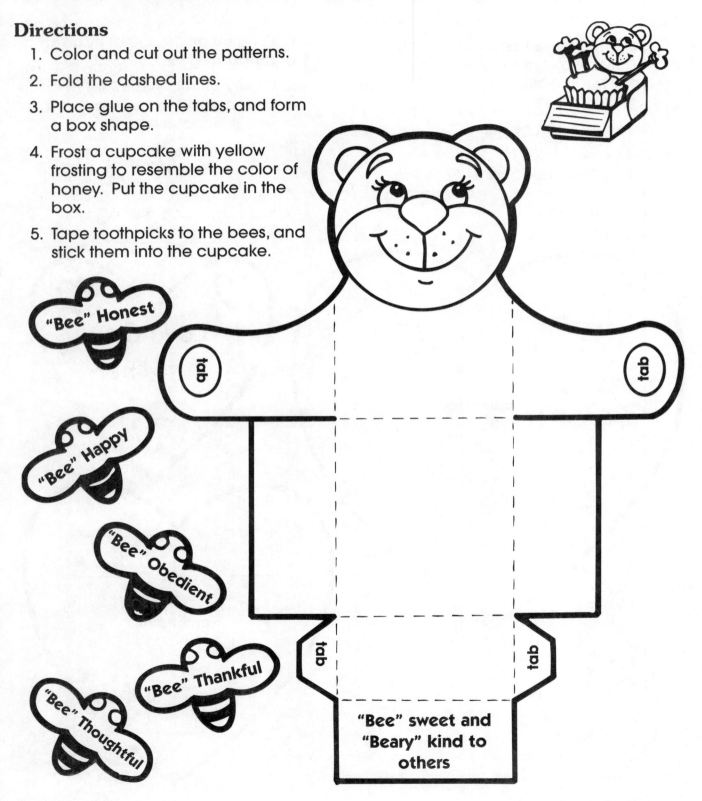

"Bee" Honest

"Bee" Happy

"Bee" Obedient

"Bee" Thankful

"Bee" Thoughtful

tab

tab

tab

tab

"Bee" sweet and "Beary" kind to others

God's Care Birdhouse

"So don't be afraid; you are worth more than many sparrows." (Matthew 10:31)

This cute birdhouse is a good reminder that we should help take care of God's small creatures.

Directions

1. Color and cut out the patterns.
2. Fold on the dashed lines.
3. Apply glue to the tabs on the birdhouse and glue to make the house. (Do not glue down roof of birdhouse.)
4. Glue the bird to the house.
5. Fill with candies, crayons, or other items.

God Made the World

In the beginning God created the heavens and the earth. (Genesis 1:1)

God made our beautiful world, and this picture is a nice reminder of His creation.

Directions

1. Color the picture below.

2. Cut out the picture on the bold lines. Glue it to a sheet of construction paper.

3. Glue fluffed-up cotton balls in the dashed areas to resemble clouds.

In the beginning God created the heavens and the earth. (Genesis 1:1)

Day and Night

"As long as the earth endures, seedtime and harvest, cold and heat, summer and winter, day and night will never cease." (Genesis 8:22)

God made our world to run perfectly. What a nice way to learn where it is day and where it is night!

Directions

1. Color and cut out the patterns.

2. Cut a slit in the center of pattern B.

3. Insert a brass fastener into the center dot of pattern A and then into the center dot on pattern B.

4. Put ½ of A into the slot of B.

5. Turn A to see "day" and "night."

"A"

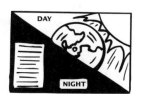

"B"

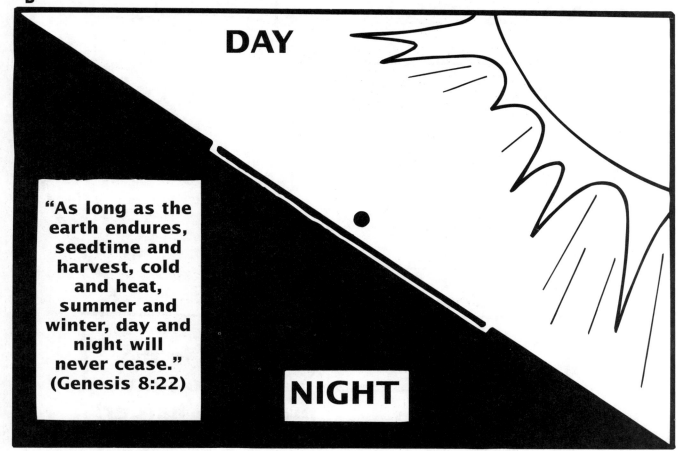

DAY

"As long as the earth endures, seedtime and harvest, cold and heat, summer and winter, day and night will never cease." (Genesis 8:22)

NIGHT

Prayer Request Reminder

*Hear my voice when I call, O Lord;
be merciful to me and answer me.*
(Psalm 27:7)

Keep this handy reminder in
your Bible as a bookmark to
remind yourself to pray
for others.

Directions

1. Cut out on the bold lines.
2. Fold on the dashed lines.
3. Apply glue to the back of
   the hands and glue
   together.
4. Fill out the requests.

**Special Prayer
Request Reminder**

1._____
2._____
3._____
4._____
5._____
6._____
7._____
8._____
9._____
10._____
11._____
12._____

**When it is the
hardest to pray—
pray even harder!**

Noah's Ark Turnaround

The Lord then said to Noah, "Go into the ark, you and your whole family, because I have found you righteous in this generation." (Genesis 7:1)

Noah's ark was filled with two of all God's creatures. This craft is a fun way to see some of them.

Directions

1. Color the pattern below and on page 78.

2. Cut out the patterns on the bold lines, and cut out the window.

3. Insert a brass fastener into the center black dot of the ark. Then put the brass fastener into the center black dot in the circle pattern. Turn to see the pictures.

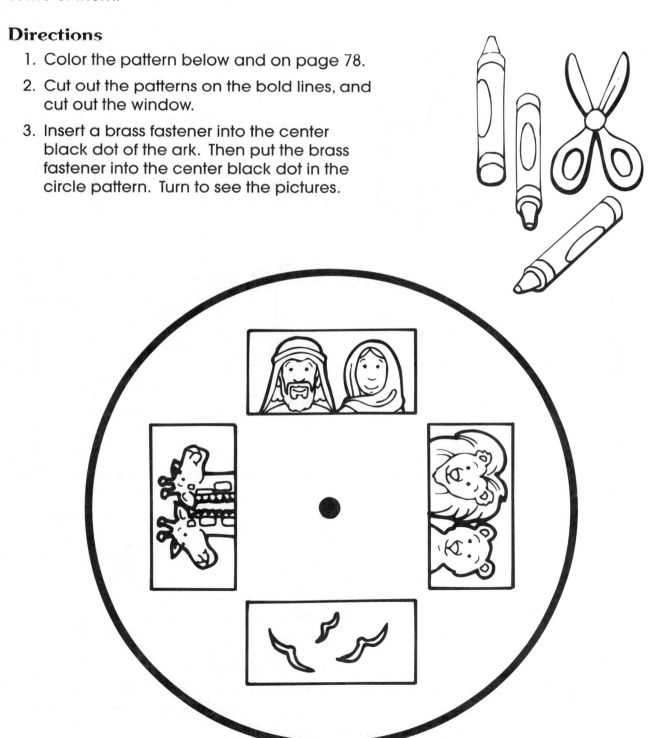

Noah's Ark Turnaround

Cut out.

Obey God and He will take care of you!

78

God's Promises Picture

"I have set my rainbow in the clouds, and it will be the sign of the covenant between me and the earth." (Genesis 9:13)

This craft can help us remember God's promise to us—that He will never again destroy the earth.

Directions

1. Color the pattern below and on page 80.
2. Cut them out on the bold lines.
3. Fold on the dashed lines.
4. Put glue on the tabs on the rainbow.
5. Glue the rainbow tabs to the base of the forest scene and stand it up.

The Promises of God Are Sure

God's Promises Picture

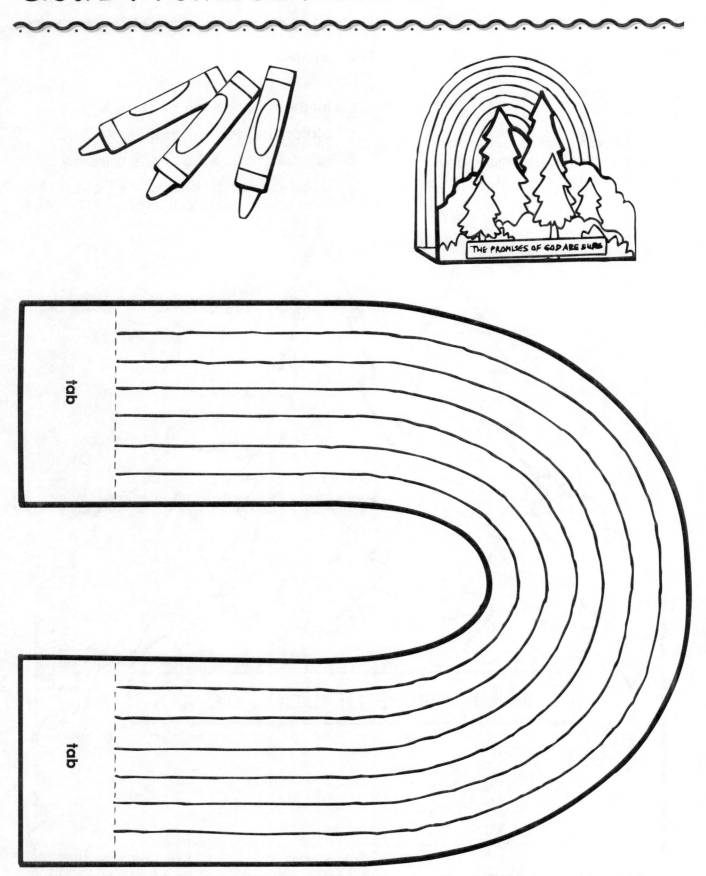

tab

tab

Light of Life Lighthouse

When Jesus spoke again to the people, he said, "I am the light of the world. Whoever follows me will never walk in darkness, but will have the light of life." (John 8:12)

This lighthouse is the perfect way to let others know that Jesus is the Light!

Directions

1. Color and cut out the pattern.
2. Fold on the dashed lines.
3. Apply glue to the tab, and fasten to form a tube shape.
4. Stand it up.

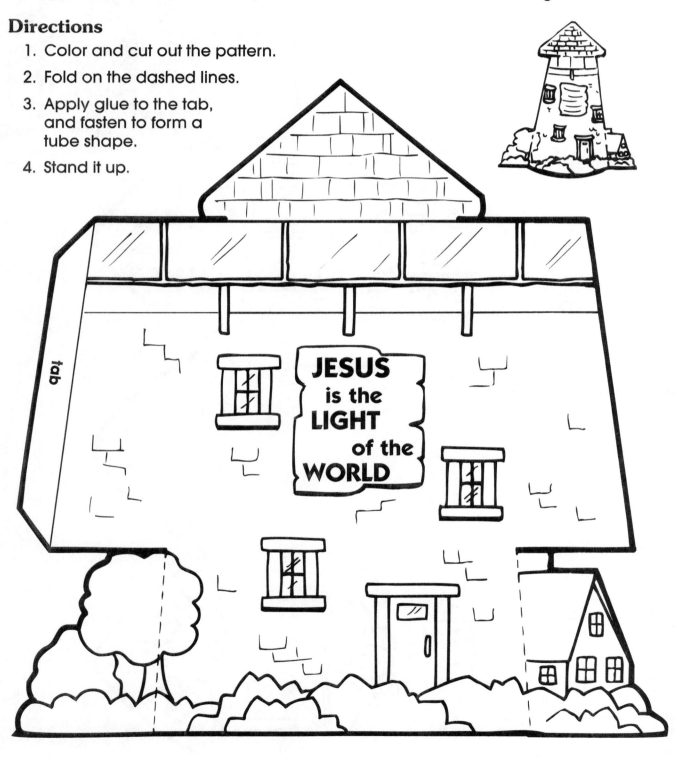

tab

JESUS is the LIGHT of the WORLD

A Dream of Heaven

. . . "I tell you the truth, no one can see the kingdom of God unless he is born again."
(John 3:3)

What a wonderful way to learn about the kingdom of God!

Directions

1. Color and cut out the patterns.
2. Glue back-to-back.
3. Fold on the dashed lines.

Glue back to back.

Fold on dashed lines.

Open to reveal inside.

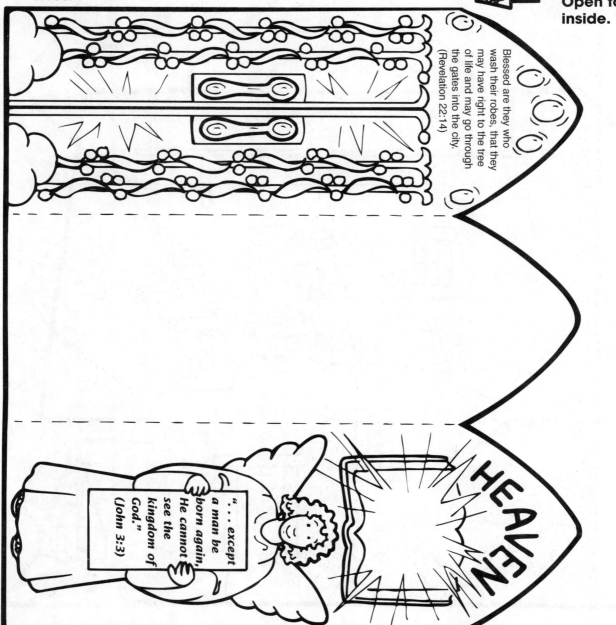

Blessed are they who wash their robes, that they may have right to the tree of life and may go through the gates into the city. (Revelation 22:14)

" . . . except a man be born again, He cannot see the kingdom of God." (John 3:3)

HEAVEN

A Dream of Heaven

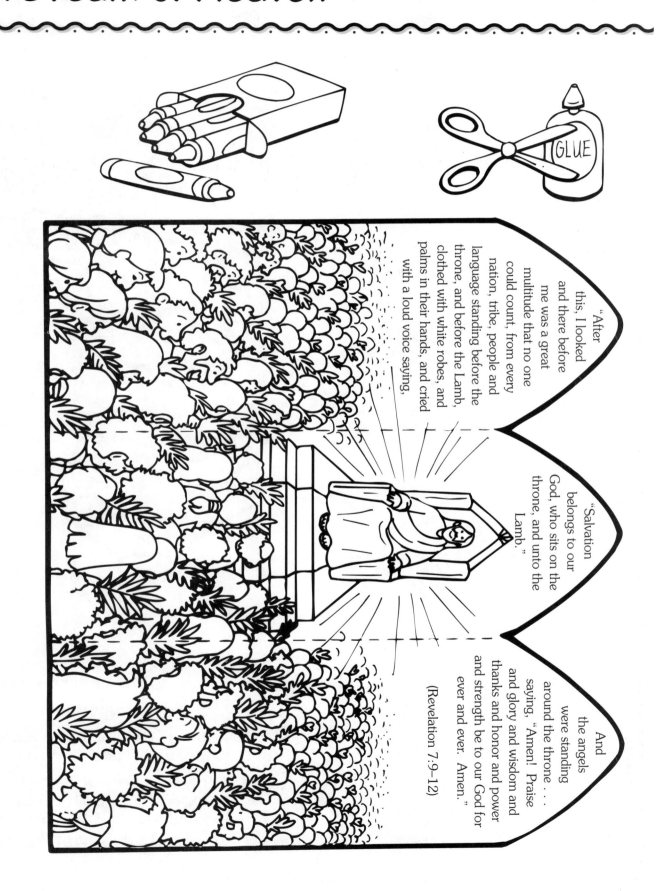

"After this, I looked and there before me was a great multitude that no one could count, from every nation, tribe, people and language standing before the throne, and before the Lamb, clothed with white robes, and palms in their hands, and cried with a loud voice saying,

"Salvation belongs to our God, who sits on the throne, and unto the Lamb."

And the angels were standing around the throne . . . and glory and wisdom and thanks and honor and power and strength be to our God for ever and ever. Amen." saying, "Amen! Praise

(Revelation 7:9–12)

Dove of Peace

Do not be anxious about anything, but in everything, by prayer and petition, with thanksgiving, present your requests to God. And the peace of God, which transcends all understanding, will guard your hearts and your minds in Christ Jesus. (Philippians 4:6–7)

This cute dove is a sign that God gives us peace.

. . . the peace of God . . . transcends all understanding . . .

tab

GOD GIVES REAL PEACE

*

Directions

1. Color and cut out the patterns.

2. Fold on the dashed lines.

3. Apply glue to the tab, and glue to the area marked with an *.

4. Apply glue behind the bird's beak, and glue both beaks together.

5. Set up or hang it up to see marked side of wings.

Sheep Mask

The Lord is my shepherd, I shall not be in want. (Psalm 23:1)

What a fun way to remember that each of us is one of God's sheep!

Directions

1. Cut out the pattern. Cut out the eye areas.

2. Glue fluffed-out cotton balls in the area marked with an *.

3. Punch out holes on the ears as indicated and tie a string to fit the mask to your head.

Optional: Glue the mask to lightweight cardboard or poster board, and cut it out again.

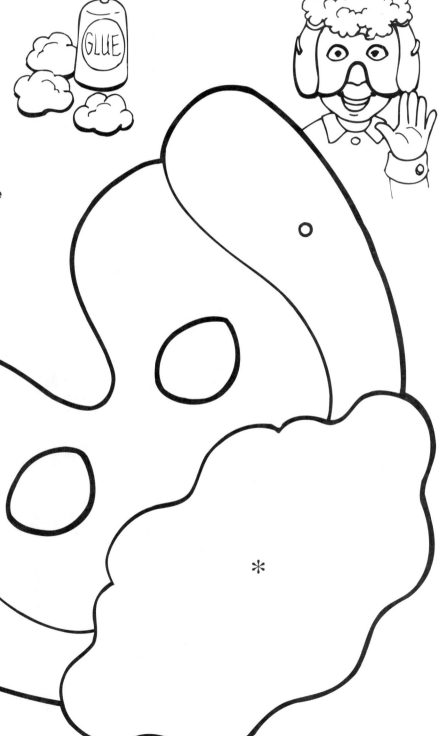

Egg and Chick Project

So God created the great creatures of the sea and every living and moving thing with which the water teems, according to their kinds, and every winged bird according to its kind. And God saw that it was good. (Genesis 1:21)

This little egg and chick craft is a fun way to remind others that God made everything!

Directions

1. Color and cut out the patterns.

2. Fold on the dashed lines.

3. Put glue on the tabs, and glue the tabs to the back side of the other half of the egg.

4. Put the little chick in the egg, and pull it out to show others.

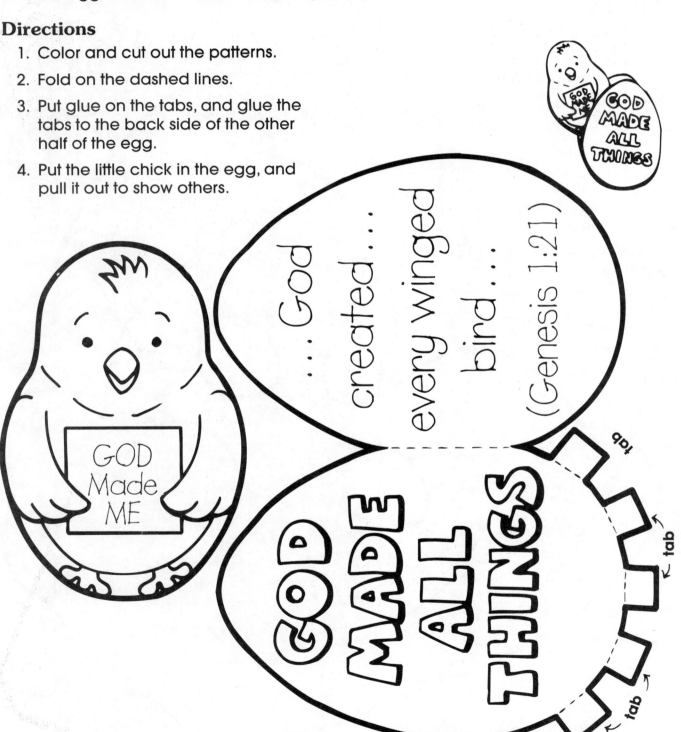

Rabbit Reminder

. . . Everyone should be quick to listen, slow to speak and slow to become angry.
(James 1:19)

What a nice way to remind us to think before we speak!

Directions

1. Color and cut out the pattern.

2. Cover the pattern with a thin layer of glue.

3. Press fluffed-out cotton balls on the sides and back of the bunny.

4. Apply glue to the tab. Roll the pattern and glue as shown.

- Listen carefully
- Speak quietly
- Do not get angry

tab

A Hungry Chick

Spring

And my God will meet all your needs according to his glorious riches in Christ Jesus. (Philippians 4:19)

This chick can help us remember that if we believe in God, He will take care of us.

Directions

1. Color and cut out the patterns.
2. Glue birdseed in the dish.
3. Insert a brass fastener in the bottom dot of the chick and then in the black dot on the picture.
4. Move the chick up and down to help it eat.

"And my God will meet all your needs according to his glorious riches in Christ Jesus." (Philippians 4:19)

"The Story of Jesus" Book

Jesus did many other things as well. If every one of them were written down, I suppose that even the whole world would not have room for the books that would be written. (John 21:25)

This book is a nice way to read and learn all about Jesus' life.

Directions

1. Color and cut out the patterns.

2. Staple the pages together to create a book about Jesus' life.

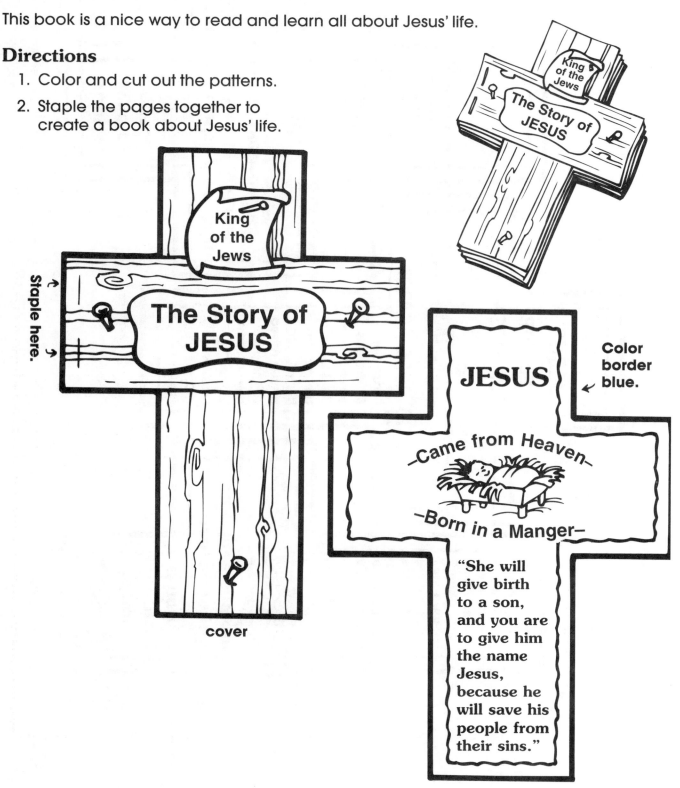

Staple here.

King
of the
Jews

The Story of JESUS

cover

JESUS

Color border blue.

-Came from Heaven-

-Born in a Manger-

"She will give birth to a son, and you are to give him the name Jesus, because he will save his people from their sins."

"The Story of Jesus" Book

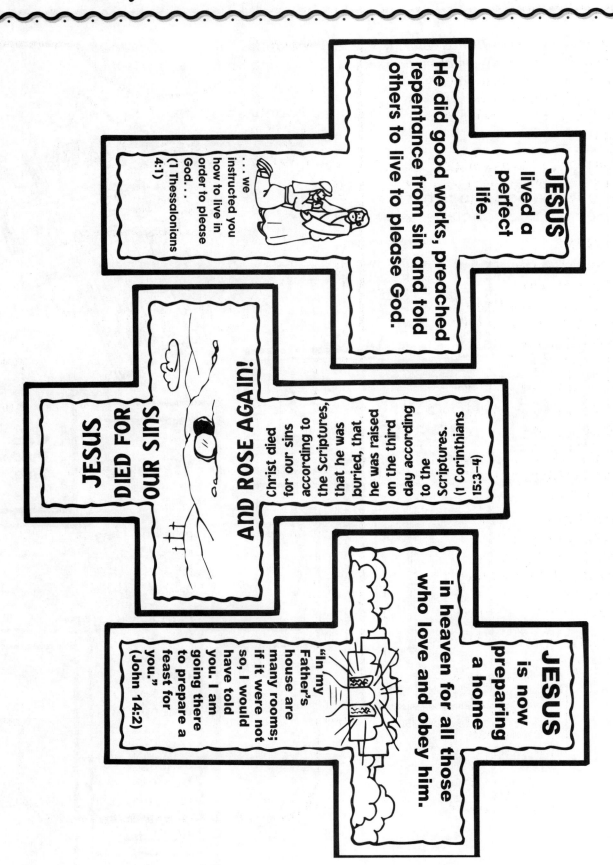

JESUS lived a perfect life.

He did good works, preached repentance from sin and told others to live to please God.

. . . we instructed you how to live in order to please God. . . . (1 Thessalonians 4:1)

JESUS DIED FOR OUR SINS AND ROSE AGAIN!

Christ died for our sins according to the Scriptures, that he was buried, that he was raised on the third day according to the Scriptures. (1 Corinthians 15:3–4)

JESUS is now preparing a home

in heaven for all those who love and obey him.

"In my Father's house are many rooms; if it were not so, I would have told you. I am going there to prepare a feast for you." (John 14:2)

Christian Life Coloring Box

Therefore, I urge you, brothers, in view of God's mercy, to offer your bodies as living sacrifices, holy and pleasing to God—this is your spiritual act of worship. (Romans 12:1)

This full box of "crayons" can help us look at colors and think of ways to live a Christian life!

Directions

1. Color the pattern here and the patterns on page 92. (Be sure to color the patterns the colors indicated).

2. Cut out the patterns.

3. Fold the box on the dashed lines.

4. Put glue on the tabs, and glue to form a coloring box.

5. Roll each "crayon" around a pencil. Take the pencil out, and put glue where shown. Glue to create the "crayon."

6. Put the "crayons" in the box.

Color the box yellow.

Apply glue here.

Apply glue here.

CHRISTIAN LIFE

Cut out.

COLORS

1. Dirty Black – All are born with sinful lives.
2. Repentant Brown – We should be sorry for doing wrong and want to do right.
3. Cleansing Red – Only the blood of Jesus can take away all sins.
4. Pure White – Trusting in Jesus can give us peace and a new life.
5. Growing Green – Live life for Jesus, obeying the Bible.
6. Dreaming Blue – We can think about living with Jesus.
7. Heavenly Yellow – When we reach heaven, we can live there forever with Jesus.

CHRISTIAN LIFE COLORS

Christian Life Coloring Box

Apply glue here.

Dirty Black

All are born with sinful lives.

Apply glue here.

Repentant Brown

We should be sorry for doing wrong and want to do right.

Apply glue here.

Cleansing Red

Only Jesus' blood can take away all sin.

Apply glue here.

Pure White

Trusting in Jesus can give us peace.

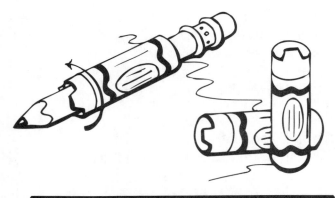

Apply glue here.

Growing Green

We should live according to God's Word.

Apply glue here.

Dreaming Blue

We can look up and forward with life with Jesus.

Apply glue here.

Heavenly Yellow

We can be happy in heaven forever.

Bible Plaque

Your word is a lamp to my feet and a light for my path.
(Psalm 119:105)

This Bible is a great way to remind us to read and obey God's Word!

Directions

1. Color and cut out the pattern.

2. Fold on the dashed lines.

3. Apply glue to the tab, and glue. Stand up the "Bible."

Your word is a lamp to my feet and a light for my path.

(Psalm 119:105)

tab

Phone Number List

May the words of my mouth and the meditation of my heart be pleasing in your sight, O Lord, my Rock and my Redeemer. (Psalm 19:14)

This list can remind us to always speak kindly of others when we talk to them!

Directions

1. Color and cut out the pattern.

2. Fold on the dashed lines.

3. Apply glue behind the tabs, and glue to form a pocket as shown.

4. Tie string in the slots to hang up.

Important Phone Numbers

tab

tab

tab

May the words of my mouth be pleasing in your sight. (Psalm 19:14)

"Sing His Praises" 3-D Picture

I will sing of the Lord's great love forever; with my mouth I will make your faithfulness known through all generations. (Psalm 89:1)

This pretty picture is a perfect way to tell others to sing of God's great love.

Directions

1. Color and cut out the patterns below and the pattern on page 96.

2. Fold the flowers on the dashed lines.

3. Put glue on the back center of each flower, and glue them to the picture on the areas marked with an *. Allow flowers to stand up for a 3-D effect.

4. Punch a hole in the hanger as shown. Glue to the back of the picture.

5. Let dry and hang.

*Optional: Glue the picture and hanger on lightweight cardboard, and cut out again.

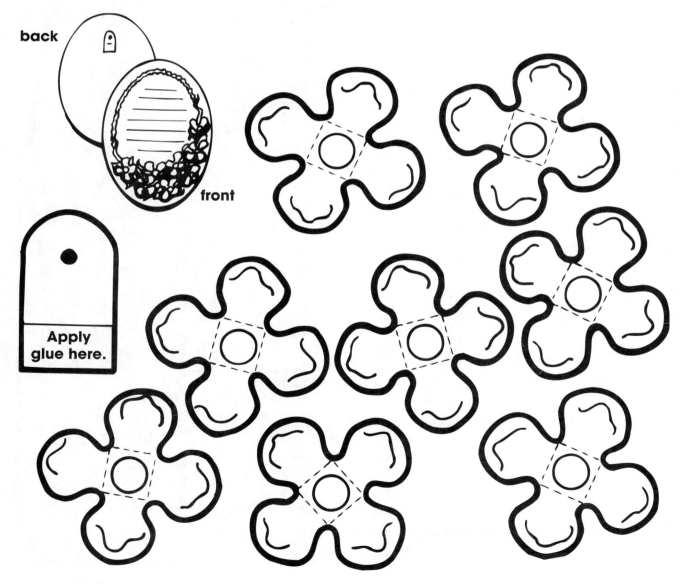

back

front

Apply glue here.

"Sing His Praises" 3-D Picture

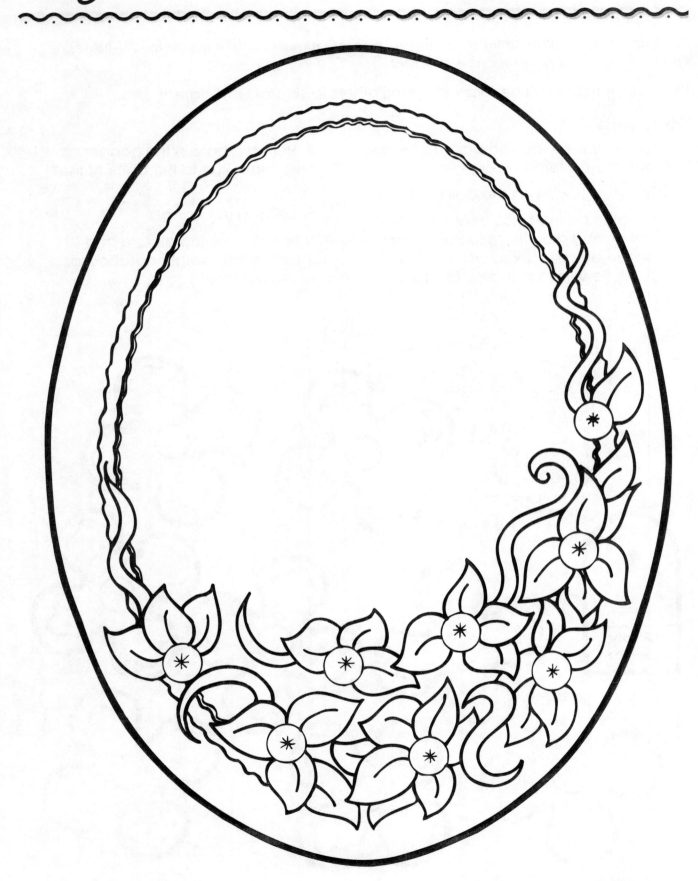

Time to Obey God

Be very careful, then, how you live—not as unwise but as wise, making the most of every opportunity, because the days are evil. (Ephesians 5:15–16)

This clock can remind all of us that now is the time to live a good Christian life!

Directions

1. Color and cut out the patterns.

2. Fold on the dashed lines.

3. Apply glue to the tab, and glue it to the area marked with an * to form a stand.

4. Insert a brass fastener in the hands and then in the center dot in the clock.

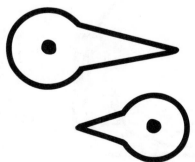

Resting Sheep

Know that the Lord is God. It is he who made us, and we are his; we are his people, the sheep of his pasture. (Psalm 100:3)

This little sheep box is perfect to use to store cotton balls or cotton swabs. It can remind us that God is our Shepherd, and we are His sheep.

Directions

1. Color and cut out the pattern below and the pattern on page 99.

2. Fold on the dashed lines.

3. Apply glue to the tabs, and glue to form a box shape.

4. Glue the sheep to the front of the box.

*Optional: Glue fluffed-up cotton balls on the sheep.

Resting Sheep

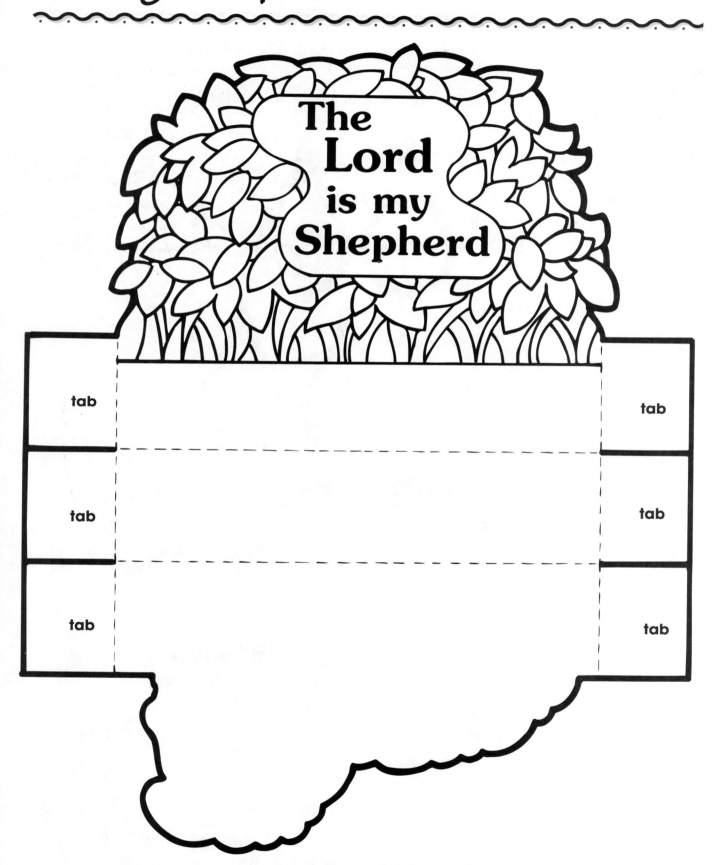

The
Lord
is my
Shepherd

tab

tab

tab

tab

tab

tab

Rain Mobile

He covers the sky with clouds; he supplies the earth with rain and makes grass grow on the hills. (Psalm 147:8)

When we hang this mobile, we can remember to thank God for the rain that makes everything grow!

Directions

1. Color and cut out the patterns.

2. Punch out the small, dark circles in the tips of the raindrops.

3. Tie the raindrops in varying lengths to a hanger.

4. Glue or tape the cloud to the hanger as shown.

5. Hang your mobile.

He covers the sky with clouds; he supplies the earth with rain and makes grass grow on the hills. (Psalm 147:8)

Pencil Topper

"For God so loved the world that he gave his one and only Son, that whoever believes in him shall not perish but have eternal life." (John 3:16)

What a nice way to remember that God loves us!

Directions

1. Color and cut out the pattern.

2. Punch two holes where shown.

3. Insert pencil.

God's House Puzzle

These things I remember as I pour out my soul: how I used to go with the multitude, leading the procession to the house of God, with shouts of joy and thanksgiving . . . (Psalm 42:4)

Creating this church can remind us to go to church and praise God.

Directions

1. Color the patterns below and the pattern on page 102.

2. Cut out the pattern below. Glue them on the church.

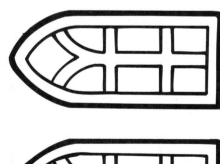

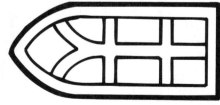

God's House Puzzle

A Basket of Flowers for Mom

. . . a woman who fears the Lord is to be praised. (Proverbs 31:30)

This little basket makes a nice gift for Mom!

Directions

1. Color and cut out the pattern.
2. Apply glue to the tabs, and glue to the areas shown to create a basket for Mom.

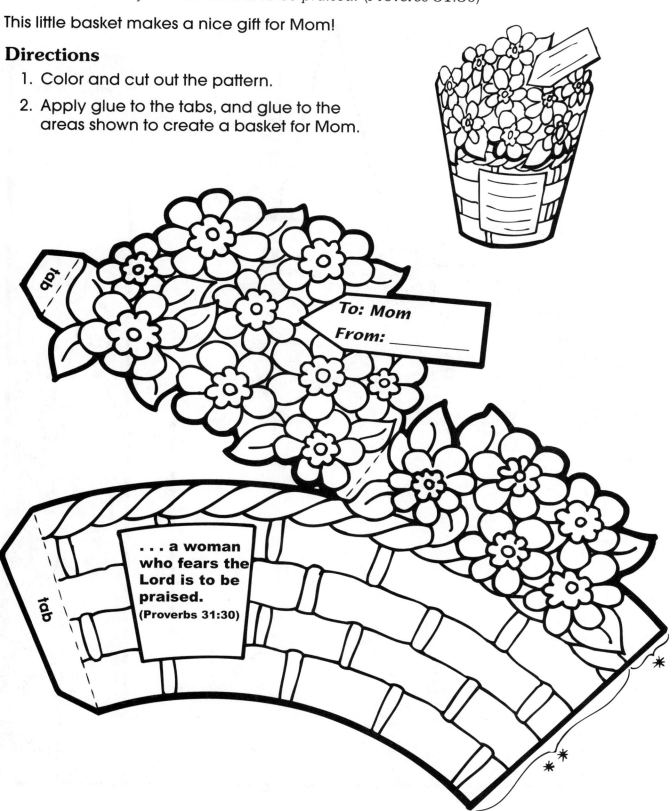

To: Mom
From: _____

. . . a woman who fears the Lord is to be praised. (Proverbs 31:30)

tab

tab

Gift Basket

The Lord is good to those whose hope is in him, to the one who seeks him.
(Lamentations 3:25)

What a sweet gift for anyone needing a smile!

Directions

1. Color and cut out the patterns.

2. Fold on the dashed lines.

3. Apply glue on the back of leaves, and glue to form a box shape.

4. Glue on the handle.

5. Fill with goodies and give to a friend.

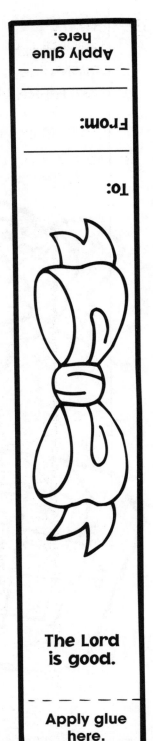

Apply glue here.

From:

To:

The Lord is good.

Apply glue here.

Helping Hands

We work hard with our own hands. (1 Corinthians 4:12)

God gave us helping hands we can use to help others!

Directions

1. Color and cut out the patterns.

2. Insert a brass fastener into the black dot on the arm and then into the girl.

3. Move the arm up and down to see her clean dishes.

We work hard with our own hands. (1 Corinthians 4:12)

Graduate Centerpiece

Let the wise listen and add to their learning . . . (Proverbs 1:5)

This little centerpiece will bring a smile to any graduate's face!

Directions

1. Color and cut out the pattern.

2. Apply glue to the tab.

3. Roll the pattern to form a cone shape. Position the graduate upright.

*Optional: Enlarge the pattern to create a table centerpiece.

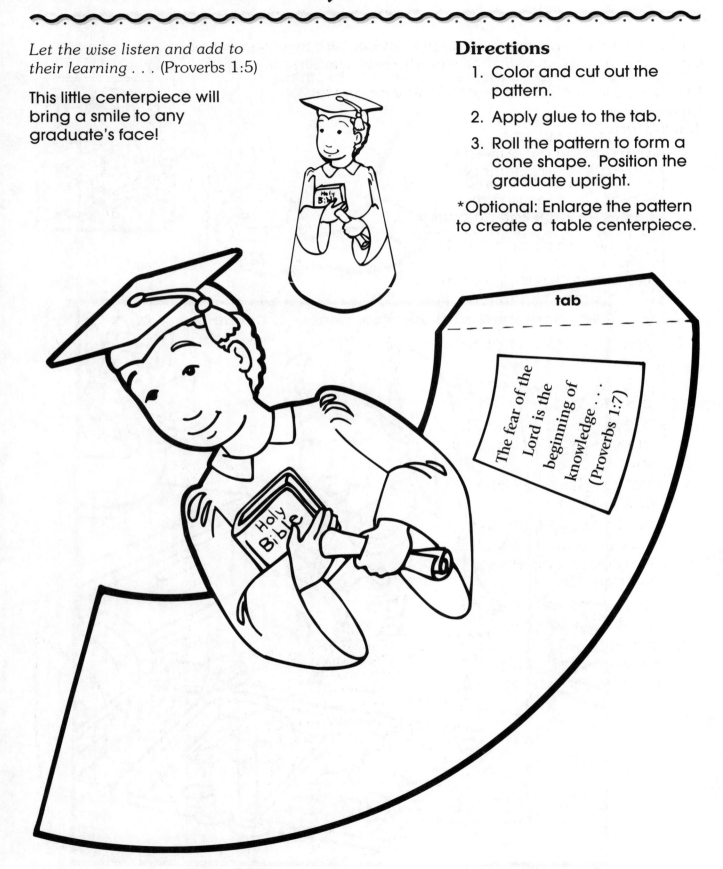

tab

The fear of the Lord is the beginning of knowledge . . . (Proverbs 1:7)

Holy Bible

Spring Centerpiece

And without faith it is impossible to please God, because anyone who comes to him must believe that he exists and that he rewards those who earnestly seek him. (Hebrews 11:6)

This centerpiece makes a pretty display for any table!

Directions

1. Color and cut out pattern A below and the patterns on pages 108–110.

2. Apply glue to the tab on pattern D. Roll to form a cone shape, and glue.

3. Glue pattern A (below) on the cone. (See the illustration to the right.)

4. Make the daffodil flowers as follows:

   • Fold all patterns B's on the dashed lines.

   • Apply glue to the tabs. Then glue the tabs to form a cup shape.

   • Roll the petals of each flower down.

   • Fold all pattern C's on the dashed lines. Apply glue to the tabs, and glue as indicated by the *.

   • Glue pattern C on to the center of pattern B.

5. Glue the flowers to the areas marked on the cone (pattern D).

"A"

And without faith it is impossible to please God, because anyone who comes to him must believe that he exists and that he rewards those who earnestly seek him. (Hebrews 11:6)

Spring Centerpiece

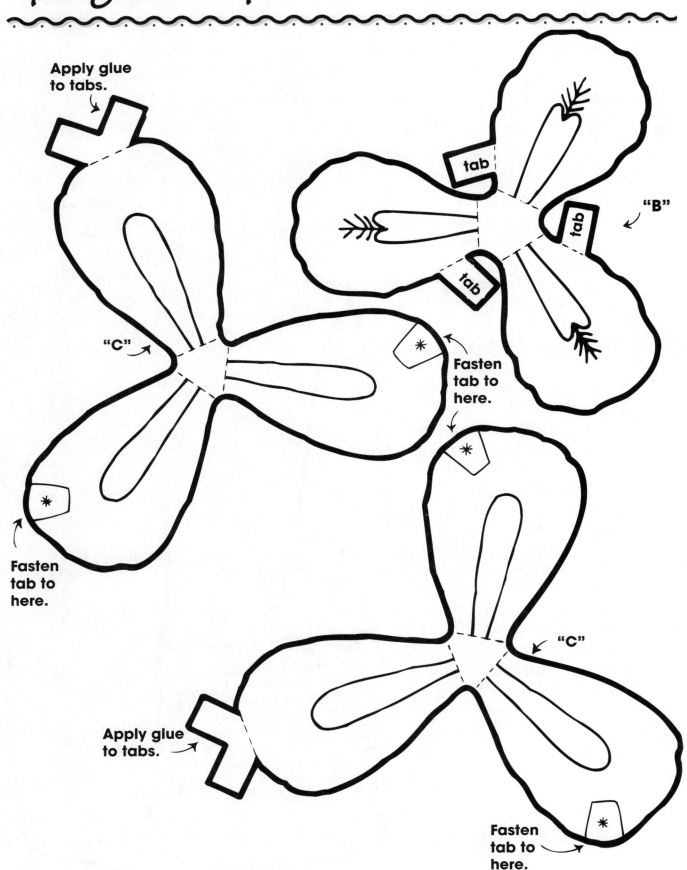

Apply glue to tabs.

tab

tab

tab

"B"

"C"

Fasten tab to here.

*

*

Fasten tab to here.

*

"C"

Apply glue to tabs.

Fasten tab to here.

*

Spring Centerpiece

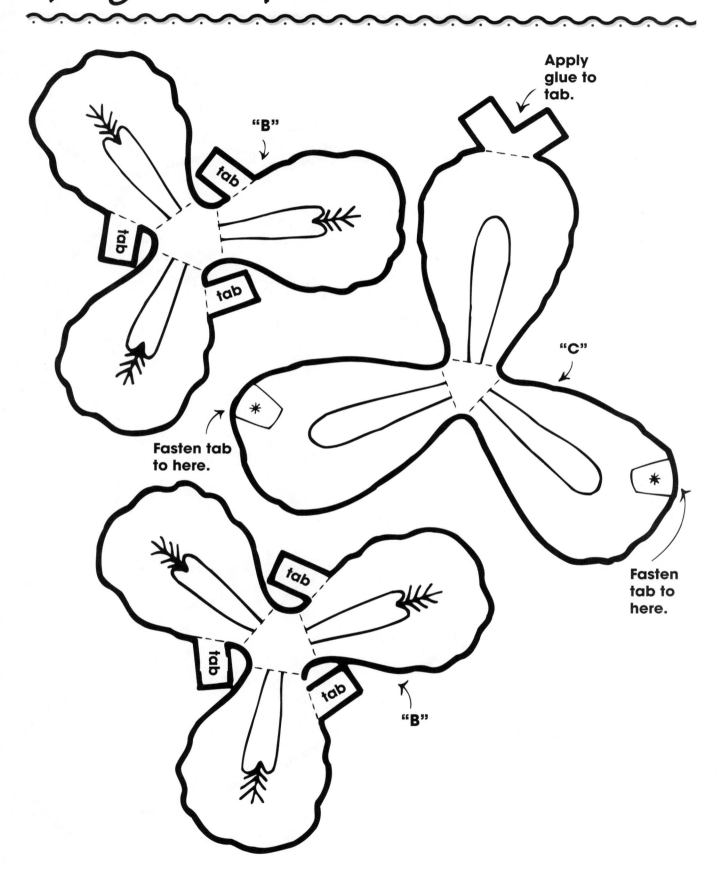

Apply glue to tab.

"B"

tab

tab

tab

"C"

Fasten tab to here.

Fasten tab to here.

tab

tab

tab

"B"

Spring Centerpiece

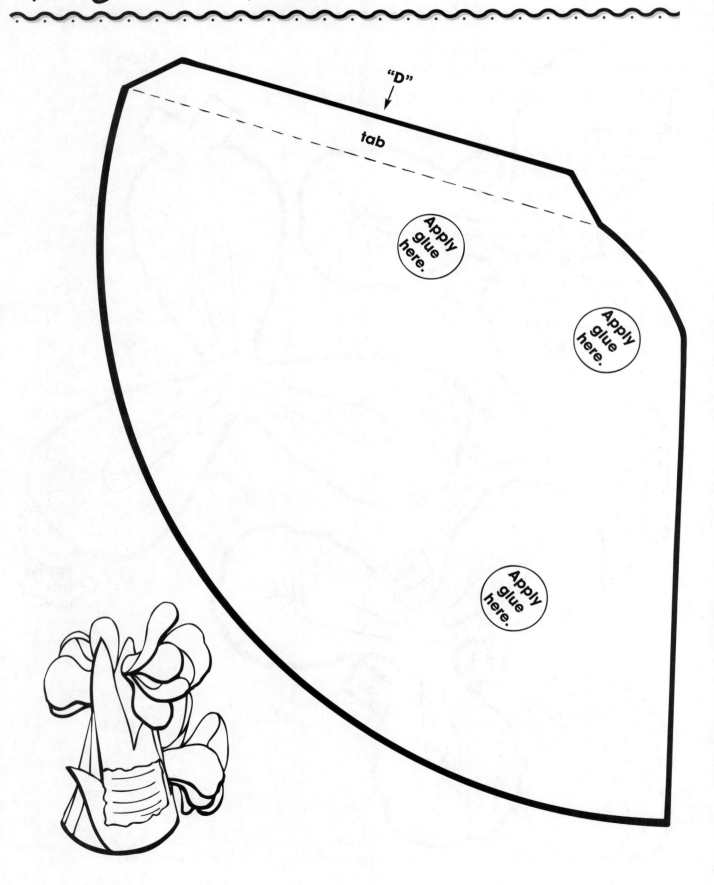

"D"

tab

Apply glue here.

Apply glue here.

Apply glue here.

Character Garden

But grow in the grace and knowledge of our Lord and Savior Jesus Christ. To him be glory both now and forever! Amen. (2 Peter 3:18)

What a cute way to help us add positive character traits to our lives!

Directions

1. Color and cut out the patterns below and the pattern on page 112.

2. Fold back and forth on the dashed lines to create a fan shape.

3. Apply glue where shown to form two pockets.

4. Insert the plants.

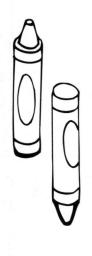

Character Garden

PRAYER

GOD'S WORD

glue

glue

glue

glue

But grow in the grace and knowledge of our Lord and Savior Jesus Christ. To him be glory both now and forever! Amen.
(2 Peter 3:18)

"Storm at Sea" Circle

But Jesus immediately said to them:
"Take courage! It is I. Don't be afraid."
(Matthew 14:27)

This circle craft is a fun way to see the kind of storm Jesus' disciples experienced!

Directions

1. Color and cut out the pattern below and the pattern on page 114.

2. Insert a brass fastener into the center dot of pattern A and into the center dot of pattern B. Turn.

"A"

Cut out.

But Jesus immediately said to them: "Take courage! It is I. Don't be afraid." (Matthew 14:27)

"Storm at Sea" Circle

"B"

114

Knock, Knock!

"Here I am! I stand at the door and knock. If anyone hears my voice and opens the door, I will come in and eat with him, and he with me." (Revelation 3:20)

This craft is a great way to remind us that if we only open our hearts to Jesus, He will come right in and stay!

Directions

1. Color and cut out the pattern.

2. Fold on the dashed lines.

3. Glue B to the back of A.

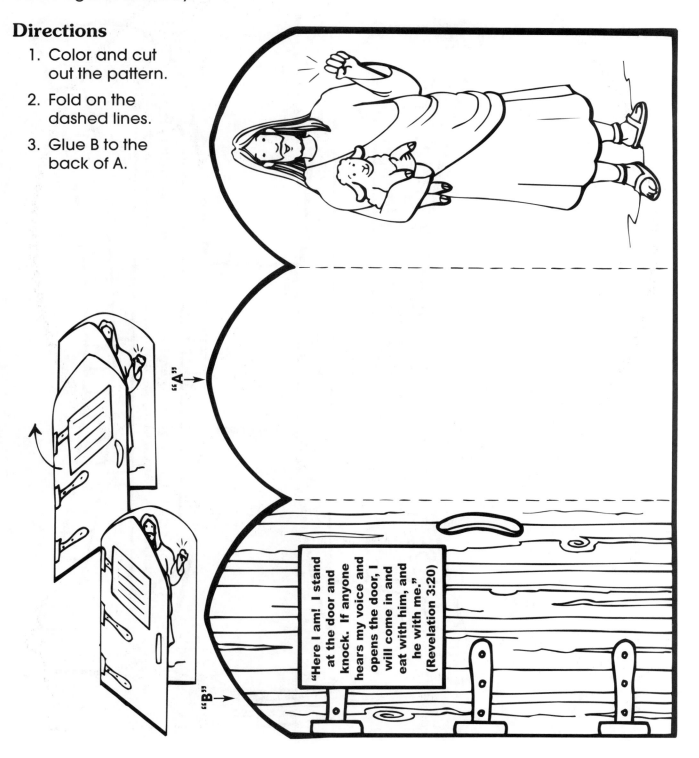

"A"

"B"

"Here I am! I stand at the door and knock. If anyone hears my voice and opens the door, I will come in and eat with him, and he with me." (Revelation 3:20)

#7101 Bible Crafts

Canoe Name Plate

Be very careful, then, how you live—not as unwise but as wise, making the most of every opportunity . . . (Ephesians 5:15–16)

God wants us to make the most of each day. This name plate can remind us to do just that!

Directions

1. Color and cut out the patterns.

2. Fold on the dashed lines.

3. Apply glue behind the ends of both canoes, and glue together.

4. Set the oars in the boat, and set the boat on a desk.

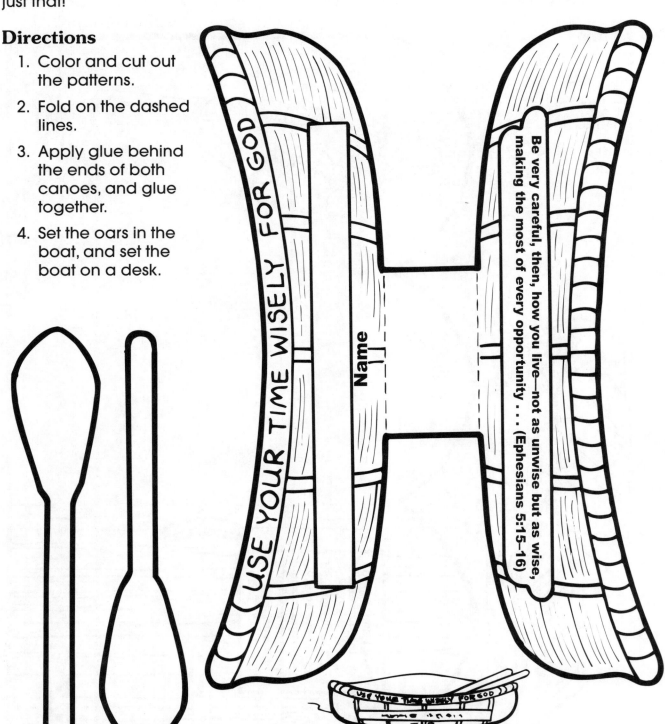

USE YOUR TIME WISELY FOR GOD

Name

Be very careful, then, how you live—not as unwise but as wise, making the most of every opportunity . . . (Ephesians 5:15–16)

Greeting Card

A friend loves at all times. . . (Proverbs 17:17)

This card and the one on page 118 are a nice way to tell a friend you care!

Directions

1. Color and cut out the pattern below and/or the pattern on page 118.

2. Fold on the dashed lines.

3. Write a message inside a card, and give it to a friend.

Thinking of you!

Use the code in the leaves to fill in the blanks below.

Cut here to make a bookmark.

Follow Jesus

Greeting Card

Color only the letters with dots.

Print the first letter of each
picture on the line above it.
GOD ALWAYS

Wishing You
a
Blessed
Day!

TO: _____

FROM: _____

Character Keys

Don't let anyone look down on you because you are young, but set an example for the believers in speech, in life, in love, in faith and in purity. (1 Timothy 4:12)

Directions

1. Color and cut out the key cards.
2. Punch a hole in each card.
3. Put the keys in order. Use a key ring to keep them together.

Ff forgiving

A B C Character Keys

Gg giving

Aa alert

Hh helpful

Bb brotherly

Ii interesting

Cc caring

Jj joyful

Dd dilgent

Kk kind

Ee eager

Ll loving

Character Keys

We can use these keys to make sure we live lives with strong Christian character!

Mm meek	Tt thankful
Nn neighborly	Uu upright
Oo obedient	Vv valiant
Pp patient	Ww wise
Qq quiet	Xx excellent
Rr ready	Yy yielding
Ss sincere	Zz zealous

Mail Holder

Summer

But everything should be done in a fitting and orderly way. (1 Corinthians 14:40)

This mail holder is a great way to keep notes and other mail organized.

Directions

1. Color and cut out the pattern by following the dashed lines.

2. Glue the pattern to the back of an 8"–9" (20 cm–23 cm) paper plate.

3. Cut out the pattern again, following the dashed lines.

4. Glue this to the front of another paper plate to form a pocket as shown.

5. Punch two holes at the top to hang up.

6. Tie a string through the holes and hang.

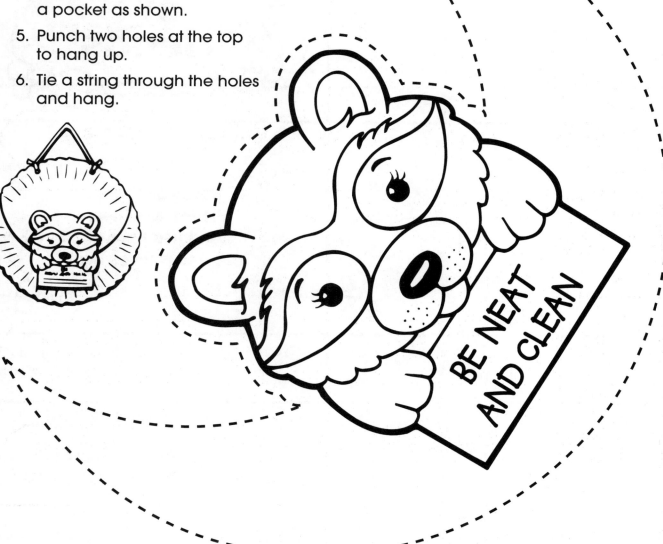

BE NEAT AND CLEAN

©*Teacher Created Materials, Inc.*   121   *#7101 Bible Crafts*

Little Autograph Album

I thank my God every time I remember you. (Philippians 1:3)

Let friends use this booklet to write short messages or Bible verses.

Directions

1. Color the pictures.
2. Cut out on the bold lines.
3. Fold on the dashed lines.
4. Slip the pages together and staple as shown.

*Optional: Add more pages.

Memories of Friends

Roses are red,
Violets are blue,
Did you know
That Jesus loves you?

Little Autograph Album

Desk Organizer

But those who hope in the Lord will renew their strength. They will soar on wings like eagles; they will run and not grow weary, they will walk and not be faint. (Isaiah 40:31)

This container is perfect to use for paper clips, nails, etc. It makes a nice Father's Day gift.

Directions

1. Color and cut out the pattern.

2. Fold on the dashed lines.

3. Apply glue to the tabs, and glue to form a box shape.

* Optional: If using it for a Father's Day gift, glue the Father's Day label to the front of the box.

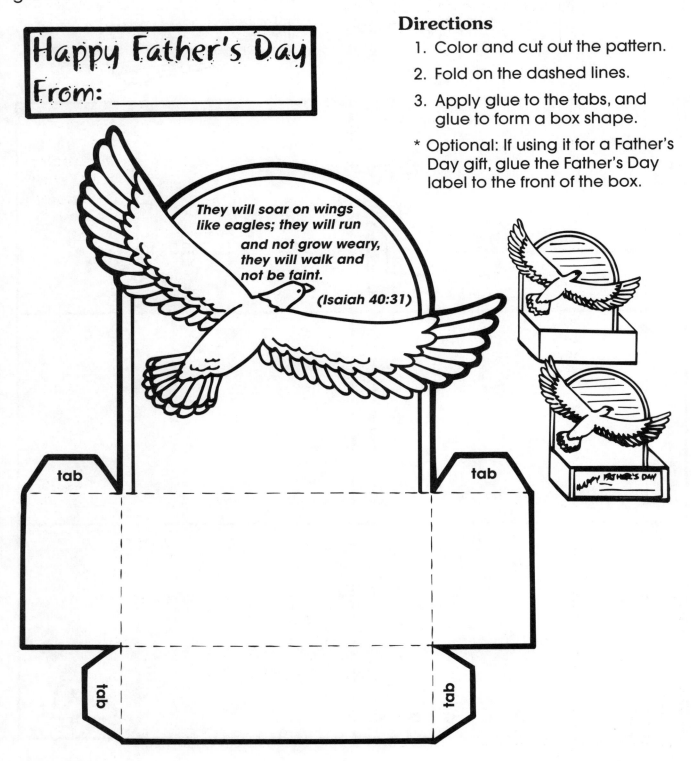

Happy Father's Day
From: _____

They will soar on wings like eagles; they will run and not grow weary, they will walk and not be faint.
(Isaiah 40:31)

tab   tab

tab   tab

Weather Vane

And he will send his angels with a loud trumpet call, and they will gather his elect from the four winds, from one end of the heavens to the other. (Matthew 24:31)

God wants us always to do our best, and this weather vane can remind us to do just that!

Directions

1. Color and cut out the patterns.
2. Cut out the slits.
3. Slip the slits together to make the rooster stand up.
4. Along the base of the weather vane, write ways you can do your best.

*Optional: Glue the pattern on lightweight cardboard for a sturdier weather vane.

North, South, East, and West— Always do your very best.

Computer Corner Sitter

"Therefore I tell you, do not worry about your life, what you will eat or drink; or about your body, what you will wear. Is not life more important than food, and the body more important than clothes?" (Matthew 6:25)

This little decoration can help us relax and remember that we need to enjoy life each day.

Directions

1. Color and cut out the pattern.

2. Fold on the dashed lines.

3. Apply glue to the tabs, and glue as shown.

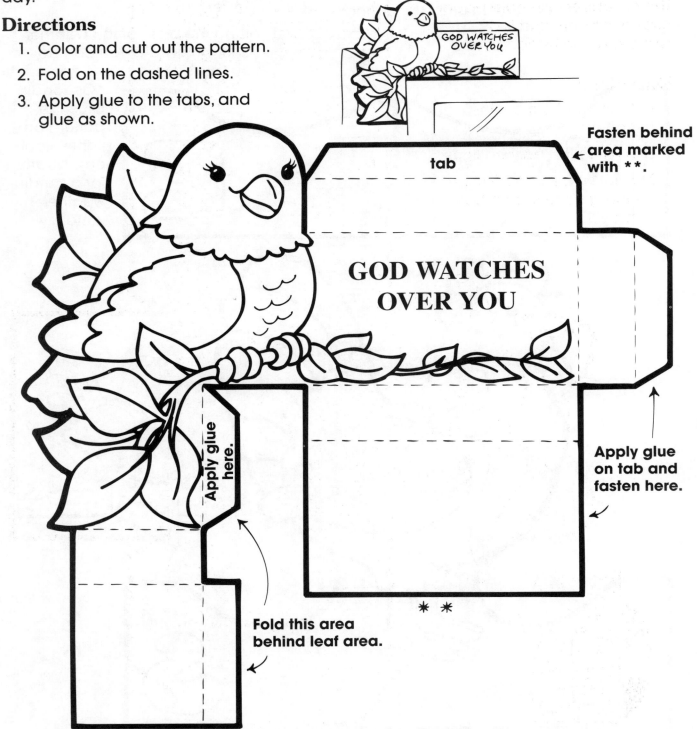

Fasten behind area marked with **.

tab

GOD WATCHES OVER YOU

Apply glue on tab and fasten here.

Apply glue here.

Fold this area behind leaf area.

* *

Raccoon Desk Organizer

Make it your ambition to lead a quiet life, to mind your own business and to work with your hands, just as we told you . . .
(1 Thessalonians 4:11)

This organizer can hold paper clips or erasers and is a wonderful motivational tool.

Directions

1. Color and cut out the pattern.

2. Fold on the dashed lines.

3. Apply glue to the tabs, and glue to form a box shape.

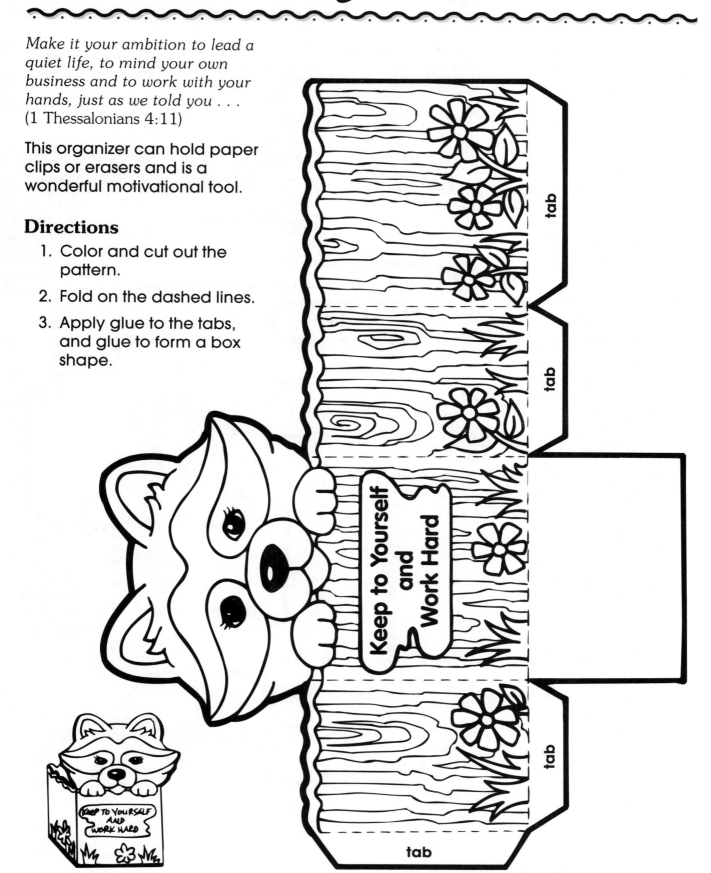

Keep to Yourself and Work Hard

tab

tab

tab

tab

#7101 Bible Crafts

Duck Pencil Holder

The Lord . . . will satisfy your needs . . . (Isaiah 58:11)

This handy pencil holder is the perfect way to remind us that God will take care of us! (Use in conjunction with the fish desk decoration on page 129.)

Directions

1. Color the pattern.
2. Cut out the pattern on the bold lines, and cut out the center hole.
3. Fold on the dashed lines.
4. Print your name in the box.
5. Apply glue to the tab, and glue the tab to the area marked with an *.
6. Set up, and lay pencils inside.

Desk Decoration

He provides food for those who fear Him; He remembers His covenant forever.
(Psalm 111:5)

This fish decoration will look great on anyone's desk! (Use it in conjunction with the duck pencil holder on page 128.)

Directions

1. Color and cut out the patterns.
2. Fold on the dashed lines.
3. Apply glue to the tab and glue the tab to the area marked with a "*" to form a stand.
5. Glue the fish on the stand where marked. (Make sure that the area on the stand is completely covered with glue as most of the fish is not glued to the stand.)
6. Let dry and set up.

*Optional: Glue the patterns to lightweight cardboard before gluing them together.

Life Compass

. . . set your hearts on things above, where Christ is seated at the right hand of God. Set your minds on things above, not on earthly things. (Colossians 3:1–2)

This compass can show us what each of us needs to do to be a good Christian no matter where we go!

Directions

1. Color the patterns.
2. Cut them out on the bold lines.
3. Fold on the dashed lines.
4. Glue the top part of the compass to the middle part as shown. (Put glue only on the edges of the pattern.)
5. Cut out the slot on the top part of the compass.
6. Insert a small brass fastener through the dot on pattern A, and then into the center on pattern B.
7. Insert the stem into the slot to close.

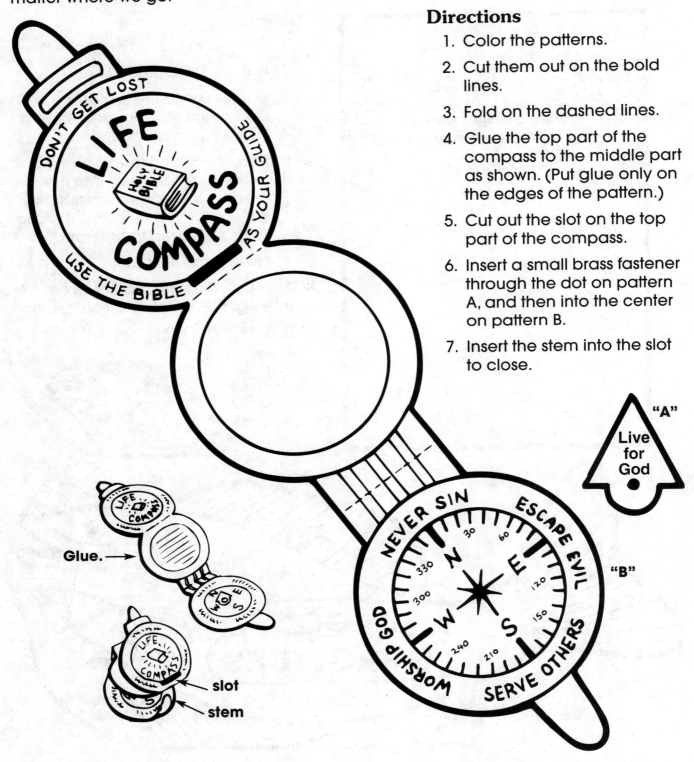

Cloud Surprise

"Heaven is my throne, and the earth is my footstool . . ." (Acts 7:49)

This craft can remind us to live a good Christian life on Earth so that we can one day live in God's kingdom—heaven.

Directions

1. Color and cut out the pattern.

2. Fold on the dashed line.

3. Apply a thin layer of glue to the back of the top half of the pattern (behind the Bible verse). Press fluffed-out cotton balls all over the glued area to resemble a cloud.

5. Open the pattern to show heaven.

*Optional: Sprinkle gold glitter all over heaven after the pattern has been colored.

"Heaven is my throne, and the earth is my footstool . . ." (Acts 7:49)

Heaven

My Goal

Obey Banner

Children, obey your parents in the Lord, for this is right. (Ephesians 6:1)

We can't forget to obey when we see this banner hanging on the wall!

tab

Directions

1. Color and cut out the patterns.
2. Glue the two strips together to form one long strip.
3. Glue the letters on the strip.
4. Hang.

OBEY

OBEY O GOD

OBEY DAD

OBEY AUTHORITY

OBEY MOM

Soldier Stand-Firm

Stand firm then, with the belt of truth buckled around your waist, with the breastplate of righteousness in place, and with your feet fitted with the readiness that comes from the gospel of peace. (Ephesians 6:14–15)

Stand up this soldier for all to see. It is a good motivator to help us stand strong in our faith.

Directions

1. Color and cut out the pattern.

2. Fold on the dashed lines.

3. Apply glue to the tab, and glue to create a triangle tube shape.

4. Stand up.

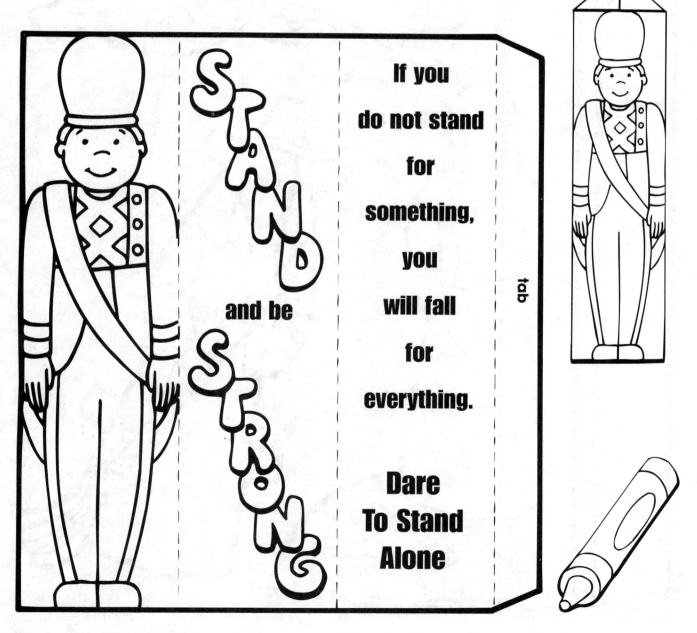

STAND and be STRONG

If you do not stand for something, you will fall for everything.

Dare To Stand Alone

tab

Esther Paper Doll

. . . And Esther won the favor of everyone who saw her. (Esther 2:15)

This doll is perfect to use to retell the story of Esther saving her people.

Directions

1. Color and cut out the patterns.

2. Fold on the dashed lines.

3. Put clothes on the doll.

*Optional: Glue the doll onto lightweight cardboard, and cut out again.

Cut out.

ESTHER

Christian Flag

Repent, then, and turn to God, so that your sins may be wiped out, that times of refreshing may come from the Lord. (Acts 3:19)

This flag can remind us all to put God first in our lives!

Directions

1. Color the cross red and the square around it blue. Leave the rest of the flag white.

2. Cut out the flag.

3. Tape a drinking straw to the lefthand side for a pole.

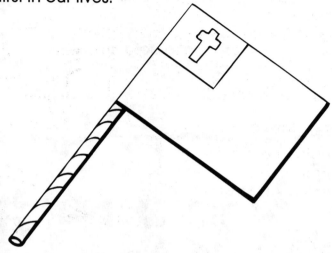

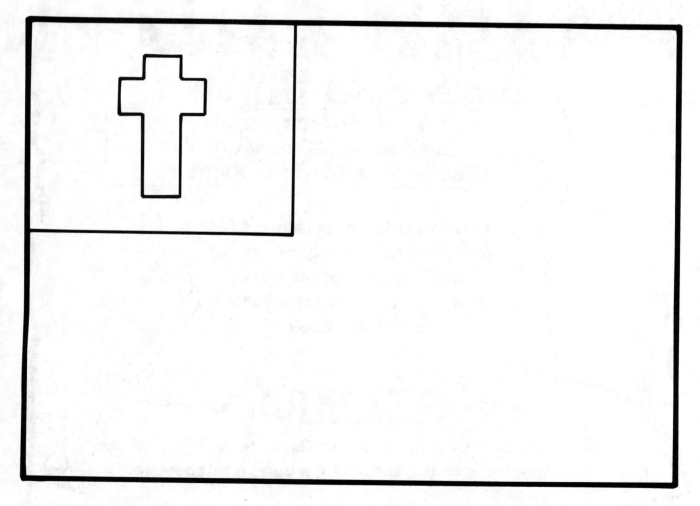

. . . the gift of God is eternal life in Christ Jesus our Lord. (Romans 6:23)

This poster is a great way to let others know that God will reward us with eternal life if we live according to His Word.

Directions

1. Use a brown crayon to color the edges of the poster.
2. Cut the poster out.
3. Glue the poster to a sheet of brown construction paper.
4. Hang it up for all to enjoy.

WANTED

BOYS AND GIRLS

**Armed with the Truth.
Loaded with Character.
Ready to Defend the Right.**

Often found standing alone for "old-fashioned," biblical morals; not following the trend of the day when contrary to gody living. The Bible is their guide book.

→ REWARD ←

GOD will give the reward. He promises eternal life to those who endure to the end, living a pure, righteous life.

Girl Paper Bag Puppet

. . . man does not live on bread alone but on every word that comes from the mouth of the Lord. (Deuteronomy 8:3)

This paper bag puppet and the one on page 138 are fun to use to share Bible stories with others.

Directions

1. Color and cut out the pattern.

2. Glue it to the bottom of a paper lunch bag.

Cut through mouth.

Boy Paper Bag Puppet

. . . man does not live on bread alone but on every word that comes from the mouth of the Lord. (Deuteronomy 8:3)

This paper bag puppet and the one on page 137 are fun to use to share Bible stories with others.

Directions

1. Color and cut out the pattern.

2. Glue it to the bottom of a paper lunch bag.

Cut through mouth.

"Jesus Cares" Suncatcher

Keep me as the apple of your eye; hide me in the shadow of your wings . . . (Psalm 17:8)

This suncatcher will let everyone know that Jesus cares!

Directions

1. Color the pattern with bright colors. Press firmly to completely cover the pattern.

2. Cut out on the bold lines.

3. Punch two holes where shown.

4. After coloring, use a small rag or tissue to spread about 1½ teaspoons of vegetable oil evenly over the pattern. Use a small rag or tissue to spread. Be sure to rub firmly into the paper.

5. Use a clean rag to rub off the excess oil.

6. Insert a short length of string in the holes, and tie to form a hanger.

7. Hang this suncatcher in a sunny window.

Prayer Plaque

Answer me when I call to you, O my righteous God. Give me relief from my distress; be merciful to me and hear my prayer. (Psalm 4:1)

God hears us when we pray, and this plaque can remind us to pray to Him!

Directions

1. Color and cut out the patterns.

2. Fold on the dashed line to form an easel shape.

3. Set the plaque on the easel.

*Optional: Glue the patterns to lightweight cardboard and cut out again.

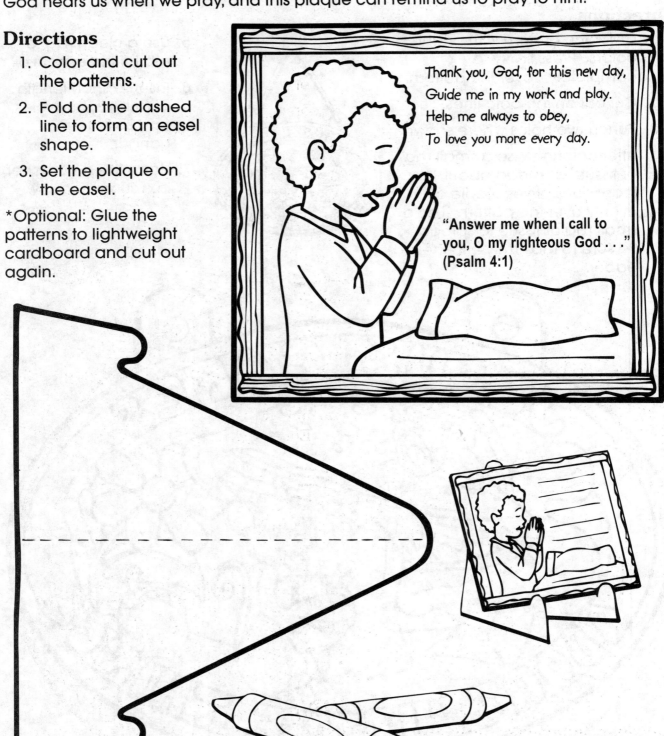

Thank you, God, for this new day,
Guide me in my work and play.
Help me always to obey,
To love you more every day.

"Answer me when I call to you, O my righteous God . . ." (Psalm 4:1)

140

"Be Strong" Fan

Then we will no longer be infants . . . blown here and there by every wind . . . Instead, . . . we will . . . grow up into him who is the . . . Christ. (Ephesians 4:14–15)

Use the fan to remind everyone that as we grow, we need to learn to be strong Christians.

Directions

1. Color and cut out the pattern.

2. Glue a craft stick to the back of the pattern.

3. Let dry and then fan away!

*Optional: Glue the fan on lightweight cardboard and cut out again.

Then we will no longer be infants . . . blown here and there by every wind . . . Instead, . . . we will . . . grow up into him who is the . . . Christ. (Ephesians 4:14–15)

Seasons Reminder

"... He has shown kindness by giving you rain from heaven and crops in their seasons. He provides you with plenty of food and fills your hearts with joy." (Acts 14:17)

This craft is a great way to remember how special each season is.

Directions

1. Color and cut out the pattern.

2. Fold on the dashed lines.

3. Apply glue to the tab, and glue as shown in the illustration to the left.

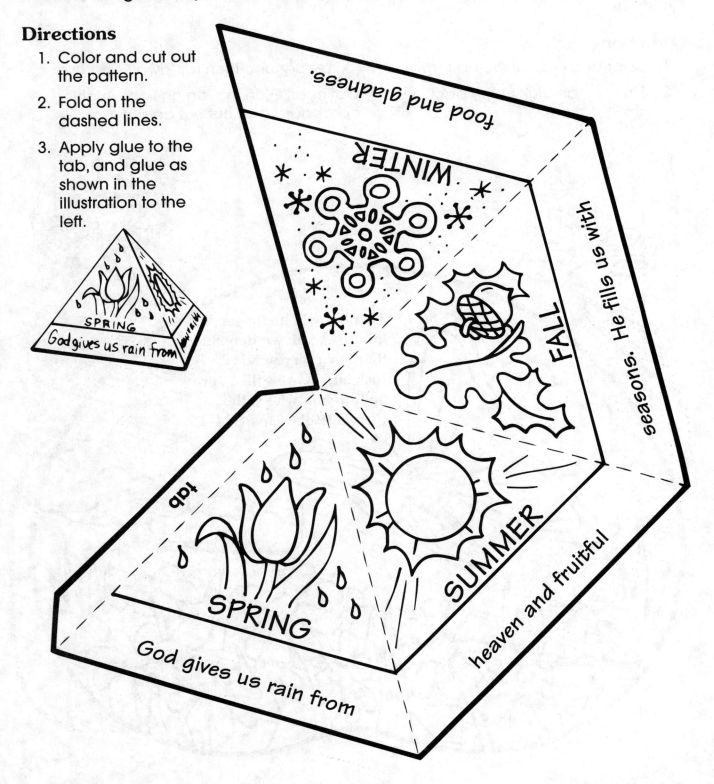

A Fantastic Fish

. . . Blessed are all who take refuge in him.
(Psalm 2:12)

This is a fun way to share the story of Jonah!

Directions

1. Color and cut out the patterns.
2. Glue patterns together as shown.
3. Fold on the dashed lines.
4. Glue Jonah inside the fish.
5. Lift the flap and show others where Jonah is.

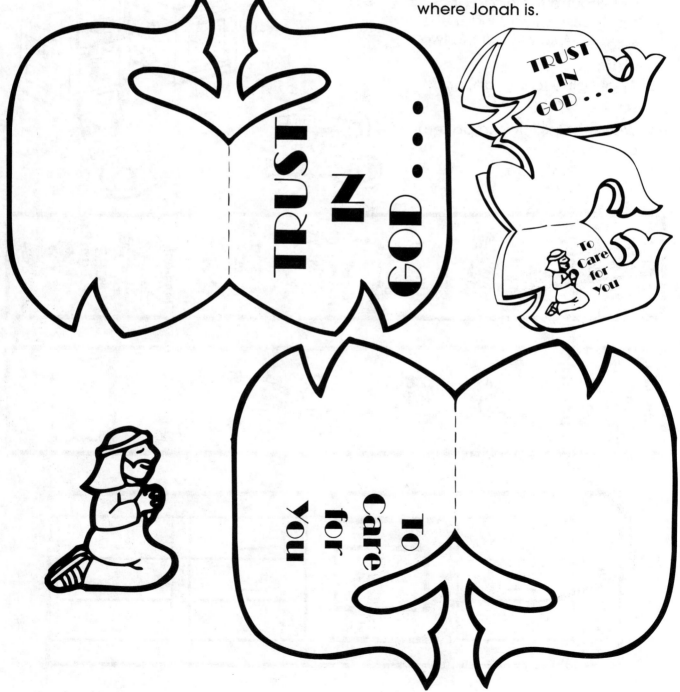

"Bee" of Good Character

Teach me to do your will, for you are my God; may your good Spirit lead me on level ground. (Psalm 143:10)

"Bee" the best Christian you can be! Always show good character.

Directions

1. Color the patterns.

2. Cut around the edge of each pattern and inside the square. Also cut out the two slots.

3. Apply glue to the tab, and glue to form a box.

4. Weave strips into the pattern as shown.

Start here.

How to "BEE" Happy | **"BEE" Saved** | **"BEE" Kind** | **"BEE" Honest** | **"BEE" Wise** | **"BEE" Obedient** | **"BEE" Thoughtful**

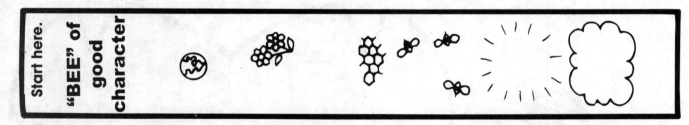

Start here.

"BEE" of good character

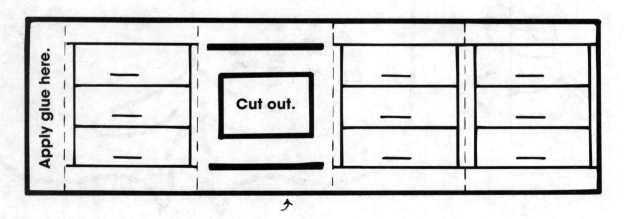

Apply glue here.

Cut out.